CHILD
ABUSE

Other Books by Elaine Landau

The Smart Spending Guide for Teens

Why Are They Starving Themselves?
Understanding Anorexia Nervosa and Bulimia

CHILD ABUSE

An American Epidemic

Elaine Landau

NORTH HIGH
SCHOOL LIBRARY

Julian Messner New York

IUPUI
UNIVERSITY LIBRARIES
COLUMBUS CENT
COLUMBUS, IN 472

Copyright © 1984 by Elaine Landau

All rights reserved including the right of
reproduction in whole or in part in any form.
Published by Julian Messner,
A Division of Simon & Schuster, Inc.
Simon & Schuster Building,
1230 Avenue of the Americas,
New York, New York 10020.
JULIAN MESSNER and colophon are trademarks of
Simon & Schuster, Inc.

10 9 8 7 6 5 4 3

Manufactured in the United States of America

Library of Congress Cataloging in Publication Data

Landau, Elaine.
   Child abuse

   Bibliography: p.
   Includes index.
   1. Child abuse—United States—Juvenile literature.
2. Child abuse—Services—United States—Juvenile
literature. I. Title.
HV741.L36   1984   362.7'044   84-996
ISBN 0-671-47988-1

For Norman Pearl

CONTENTS

NOTE FROM THE AUTHOR

This is a book about child abuse as it exists today within the American family. It deals with what factors are responsible for the creation of an abusive parent, the physical and emotional ramifications of abuse, and the unique differences that exist between child abuse and the abuse of teenagers. It is a book about families who have become destructive toward each other and what can be done to strengthen those families.

The Littlest Victims

SHERI'S STORY

Sheri May Went, a red-haired, green-eyed, seven-month-old baby girl was rushed to the emergency room of a New York City hospital by her mother, who claimed that she had been unable to rouse her little girl from the child's afternoon nap. Unfortunately, no one on the hospital staff was able to wake the baby either. Sheri had entered the hospital dead on arrival. She had been dead for over three hours. A later, more extensive examination and autopsy of the child's body revealed that the baby had died of a skull fracture and internal hemorrhaging.

When questioned about little Sheri's death, her mother could only express what appeared to be astonishment. She had no idea what could have possibly caused her baby to die, let alone suffer a skull fracture and internal bleeding. After being pressed for details, she said that her child had fallen out of the crib earlier that day while reaching down for a toy on the floor. Mrs. Went went on to relate that when she had picked Sheri up after the fall, the baby did not appear to be injured. She said that she had placed Sheri back in the crib for her afternoon nap and had only became alarmed when the child could not be woken.

That a seven-month-old baby could climb over the bars of a full-sized crib was impossible.

That little Sheri could have sustained the injuries that cost her her life even if she had taken such a fall was equally impossible.

CRAIG'S STORY

Craig died at the age of four. His parents claimed that he had fallen out of the window of their fifth-floor apartment despite their repeated warnings to him not to put his toy cars on the open windowsill. A subsequent medical examination revealed that Craig's neck had been broken before the fall. In addition, he was found to have a broken arm, several cuts and bruises, and four burn welts.

JOEY AND SUSANNA'S STORY

Three-and-a-half-year-old Joey and his seven-year-old sister Susanna burned to death in a fire at their home. The fire had started when Susanna was trying to cook dinner for herself and her little brother. The kitchen curtains touched the lighted gas stove burner and went up in flames.

The children, who were alone in the house and feared being punished by their parents for ruining the curtains, tried futilely to put out the fire themselves. By the time they tried to leave the house, it was too late. Joey never made it out the front door. Susanna died during the ambulance ride to the hospital. With her last words en route to the hospital, Susanna expressed fear that her mother would beat her for having allowed a fire to start.

Both of Susanna and Joey's parents were known alcoholics. By the time the fire occurred, the children had been left alone for over two and a half days, with almost

3

no food in the house and no money. At the time of the children's death, the authorities were unable to locate their father. Their mother was found in a bar in a neighboring town.

The list of "accidents" of which children have been the victims is lengthy. Young people have been drowned or scalded by hot water while bathing, suffocated by their own pillows while sleeping, and fallen from chairs, couches, tables, bicycles, and windows. Often, the children die. Some people have gone as far as to suggest that those were the lucky ones. Other children continue to live with an all-encompassing life-threatening kind of horror. They may have been permanently crippled or maimed, or have undergone brain damage as the result of the very severe punishments inflicted on them. All are victims of child abuse and neglect.

It is not known exactly how many children have been victims of maltreatment in America, although the most recent statistics reveal that well over 1.5 million children are abused annually. Some experts estimate that for every case of child abuse made known to the authorities, over a hundred other cases go unreported and unacknowledged. A great deal of abuse goes on in secrecy in the privacy of people's homes. Often the abusive parents do not take the child for medical treatment unless they think the child's life might be in serious danger, and they are frightened by the possible ramifications of having, perhaps unwittingly, committed a murder. In instances where the child is taken to a doctor, the parents either claim that they can't imagine how the child could have been injured or make up a very unlikely sequence of events that is hardly believable.

In an attempt to further disguise revealing scars or symptoms that might point to maltreatment, many abusive parents do not return more than once or twice to the same doctor or hospital. If asked about their child's general health or his history of accidents, the descriptions offered by parents do not always support even the most obvious conclusions drawn from x-rays and examinations. In many cases, x-rays have revealed broken bones in different stages of healing, indicating that the injuries to the child were inflicted on several occasions. The manner in which the bone is repairing itself can also provide physicians with significant information regarding the nature of the injury. Even if the parents claim that the child's arm was broken by a fall, x-rays may reveal that the bone actually snapped from being roughly twisted or pulled.

There is no doubt that child abuse exists in America today. In fact, it has been found that the incidence of abuse of children is highest in urbanized, technologically advanced societies. Unfortunately, the mistreatment of children is often a by-product of the stress generated by such highly developed environments.

We usually hear about only the most "sensationalized" cases of abuse: those that reach television, radio, and the newspapers. Stories of babies left to die in garbage cans, incinerators, and subway stations have regrettably become all too common.

However, more subtle forms of abuse take place in households across the country on a daily basis. The signs of abuse and neglect need not be a small body covered with scars or a child who has had both legs broken in numerous places. They might take the form of a child who behaves like a frightened, wounded animal shuddering at the friendly touch of another human being. A maltreated child may be someone who is severely dehydrated or on the verge of starvation. Maltreatment and neglect may also be evidenced by a child with infected sores that have not been attended to, or even by a youngster who has continually suffered from a bad case of lice.

Many children have been severely neglected by their parents or caretakers. Instances of blatant neglect may be less shocking and dramatic than those of abuse, but the effects of prolonged neglect can often be just as devastating to the young person's well being. There are many ways of neglecting a child. A parent may fail to give him adequate food, a sanitary home environment, or sufficient and appropriate clothing, or the adult may show disregard or disdain for the child's educational, medical, or emotional needs. Neglected children often are denied the necessary love, supervision, and emotional support crucial to a normal and healthy transition into adulthood.

There appears to be a tradition for the abuse and maltreatment of children set down for us through myth, history, and literature. In mythology, sacrificial altars to the gods were often stained with the blood of very young children. In ancient Greece, the eldest sons of kings were offered up as sacrifices should their own fathers' lives be threatened. The Bible contains numerous references to the destruction of young children as well. In addition to tales of children being offered up as sacrifices, there are references to laying a child's bones into the foundation of a new structure or edifice. Abraham brought his only son to the mountain, bound the child, and placed him on the sacrificial altar. The boy's life was saved only by the divine intervention of God, but there are countless stories of other children in biblical times who did not fare as well.

In ancient Mexico, newborn infants were sacrificed when maize was planted. Older children were later slain as the crops sprouted and grew. At various times ancient Greeks and Romans abandoned their infant children, often leaving them to die of exposure to the elements or be killed and eaten by wild animals. Some infants were simply cast adrift on a river. In some ancient civilizations where children served as street beggars to supplement the family income, parents might deliberately mutilate their offspring, since it was thought that a child with only one eye or a chopped-off leg might elicit more sympathy from passersby.

Even today in some regions infants may be discarded at birth if the family doesn't have sufficient food to sustain itself or in the event that the infant is born with a defect of some sort.

A baby comes into this world without the ability to care for himself. Ideally, his parents or caretakers look out for his welfare, speak up for his rights, and safeguard him from harm. When some element within this framework goes amiss and his well-being is threatened by the very people who are responsible for his protection, something must be done to help the child. Society must intervene.

The Sparks That Ignite Abuse

The abusive parent is someone who has failed in his or her role as caretaker of the child. After reading the accounts of child maltreatment that headline the front pages of newspapers, one might too easily believe that child abusers are sadists, psychotics, or crazed criminals. In reality, however, under the appropriate set of unfortunate circumstances, almost anyone might find himself or herself guilty of some degree of child abuse. Parents who fail as caretakers and mistreat their children are usually found to have had little or poor prior preparation for their role. Many of these persons were themselves abused children. They have no history of benevolent experiences and lack appropriate healthy role models after which to pattern their behavior as parents. Someone who was never given a sense of dignity and self-esteem as a young person will often experience difficulty in providing his own offspring with a sense of well-being, self-worth, and appropriate discipline.

One of the more common theories of child abuse is the hypothesis that all abused children grow up to become abusive parents. Because we learn how to parent from our own parents, it may be commonly thought that neglect breeds neglect.

However, recent research has indicated that although many abusive parents were physically beaten or hurt as children, a good number were not. Interestingly enough, the most common trait among abusive parents is that they were emotionally deprived or rejected in their youth. Many of these individuals reported never having had a "hand laid on them" as children.

Parents who were once emotionally and socially impoverished often experience a great deal of trouble learning the role of parent. Many lack insight and knowledge in dealing with infants and children, and they often express unrealistic expectations from their offspring. For example, one father severely beat his sixteen-month-old son because the boy had "messed his pants." Although a sixteen-month-old baby is too young to be toilet trained, the father had no understanding of this and interpreted his son's normal bodily functions as a challenge to his own authority. Each time the child urinated or defecated in his diaper, the father became irrationally incensed and severely beat the baby.

When any adult becomes a parent, he must undergo a definite series of changes. He must reorganize his values and priorities to now include a baby. He has to set aside the immediate gratification of his own needs, as the helpless child must now come first. Abusive parents have often been described as individuals who experience difficulty in balancing their own needs against the needs of their child.

A person who has not learned how to function as a competent parent may find a nearly intolerable situation even further aggravated by outside factors. An unwanted or unplanned pregnancy, seemingly relentless demands from older children within the family, overwork or job-related problems, financial difficulties, and countless other sources of stress may eventually help create an abusive family situation.

Seven-year-old June was the second oldest in a family

of five children. Her father worked as a busboy for minimal earnings and supported his family as best he could. June's mother was known in the neighborhood as a woman with "a drinking problem." When June's father lost his job and was unable to find another, he became depressed and agitated and eventually abandoned the family.

Unable to cope with the stress of raising five children alone and trying to make ends meet with welfare payments, June's mother began to lash out at her children. Never having been a woman who possessed a great deal of patience and tolerance for her children, her reactions grew rasher and more extreme under stress. In the past, if June played the radio too loudly and disturbed her mother's afternoon nap, her mother might have screamed and cursed at her. Lately she had taken to beating June severely with a strap with little or no provocation. Within a month of her father's departure, June's small body was covered with welts on both arms and her back.

Despite demands made on parents, child abuse could not exist in our society to the extent to which it does if some violence toward children were not deemed to be within the range of socially acceptable behavior. The way in which a culture defines the rights of children has a direct bearing on their overall treatment.

In the United States, children are still generally regarded as their parents' property. When a newborn infant leaves the hospital with his parents, the child's fate may not come to the attention of any social institution until he enters school at the age of four or five. If his parents are responsible, mature individuals who are capable of adequately meeting his needs for nurture and protection, all may go well for him. However, maltreatment problems arise when parental power is misused.

Parental authority and power are misused when they are employed to damage the child either physically or emotionally, or administered in any manner that reduces or limits the child's opportunity for normal growth and development. The absolute authority of the parent is rarely questioned in our society when it is exercised judiciously with no visible harmful side effects. The important ethical question of whether the child has a right to his own integrity as a separate individual is generally left unexamined.

A recent survey administered across the country showed that over 90 percent of parents have reported using some physical force at least once in the course of raising their children. A large proportion of mothers reported spanking infants who were under six months of age.

The use of violence against children is sanctioned to some degree by American society. Although cases of extreme physical brutality are loudly condemned by the media, when polled, numerous police, clergy, and educators have approved spanking. There is legal sanction as well for the use of force when disciplining minors. For example, in 1974 the Texas legislature enacted the following legislation: "The use of force, but not deadly force against a child younger than 18 years is justified: (1) if the actor is the child's parent or step-parent . . . (2) when and to the degree the actor believes the force is necessary to discipline the child." Laws such as this reflect the belief of some that children are the property of their parents, to be dealt with as they see fit within acceptable boundaries rather than as young citizens with an inherent sense of dignity, and needs as well as rights of their own.

A major factor that turns a disciplinary situation into one in which violence and abuse arise is often the degree to which the family finds that it is socially isolated from support networks that might be able to intervene and provide help. A parent who has not adequately adjusted to the role of caretaker and finds himself under extreme stress is far less likely to be abusive to his child if he feels able to turn to another person or a social agency for assistance. Often it need be nothing more than the opportunity to call a relative or friend to take the child out for a few hours or for a weekend. Connections may also take the form of being able to leave the child at a play group sponsored by a church or social agency while the parent relaxes, has a chance to let off some steam or gather his thoughts. When under stress, a parent may simply need to take a break from what may be, to him, an exasperating situation.

Support systems generally arise through social networks and a sense of connectedness with the community. A parent or family in trouble needs a variety of resources to call upon in times of personal crisis or excessive stress. Such resource people might include the extended family, clergy, educators, social workers, mental health practitioners, and others. Persons with a large pool of social supports and skills can draw on these resources even when they are under a great deal of stress. On the other hand, a person who is isolated and has relatively few social skills is more likely to become susceptible to abusive behavior even under considerably less stress.

Although such supports may be crucial to the normal, healthy development of children in high-risk situations, studies have shown that abusive parents usually tend to distrust and retreat from society. Parents who habitually abuse their children generally prefer not to seek help in resolving crises. In addition, abusive parents often attempt to prevent their children from forming normal, healthy relationships outside the home.

Abusive parents tend not to belong to or participate in any organized groups. A large proportion choose to have unlisted telephone numbers. A number of factors have often been found to contribute to the continuation of the abusive parent's alienation from society. Among the most common of these elements are moving, illness, the birth of a disabled child, a severe loss of income, and the loss of status that can accompany poverty.

In America, privacy and an individual's right to it have come to be a treasured commodity. However, each year hundreds of thousands of children pay for their parents' privacy through abuse and neglect.

All families need information from the outside world in order to raise their children correctly. The quality of life that a family experiences is determined not only by economic factors, but by social exchanges and positive personal interactions in the home, neighborhood, and work place. As the value of and opportunity for privacy increase, the danger of isolation from the community increases as well. When a family's isolation increases, the risk of child abuse and neglect rise correspondingly. A family climate of depression, anger, helplessness, a feeling of loss of control, and violence may be somewhat tempered by the supportive intervention of relatives or a strong tie to one's neighbors or others within the community who are willing and able to make themselves available to the stressed parent.

An isolated family does not receive proper and necessary feedback and evaluation on the development and growth of its offspring. A parent may not fully realize the effect his behavior is having on his child without comments from friends or neighbors, or a conference with the child's teacher to confirm that something is wrong.

The biological parents need not—indeed, ought not—comprise a child's sole source of love and support. The active involvement of family friends in the daily activities of the family may often prevent parental stress from being translated into violence. A relative, teacher, or friend may often provide the acceptance and understanding for the child that is lacking at home. Such individuals can also serve as positive role models after whom the child can pattern his own behavior and responses.

Timmy, now an adult, still recalls vividly how throughout his childhood he had been the victim of an abusive mother. He has never been able to forget a cruel game his mother used to play with him when he was a toddler. In this oft-repeated ritual, Timmy's mother would drop to her knees, smile lovingly, spread her arms as if she were about to embrace and hug the little boy, and say, "Timmy, come here to Mommy who loves you." When the child would run toward her, she would slap him hard across the face, often knocking him down. Leaving her toddler to cry on the floor, she would say, "That ought to teach you never to trust anyone."

Fortunately, a bright spot in Timmy's life came in the form of Stella, an upstairs neighbor, who came to function as sort of a substitute mother for Timmy throughout much of his youth. Stella was a retired actress who lived alone in the attic apartment of Timmy's building. Having never married and being without children or any family of her own, she took a liking to Timmy almost from the day he arrived home from the hospital. As a working, single parent with the responsibility of caring for two older children, Timmy's mother was quick to accept Stella's frequent offers to help care for the baby.

Stella bought a beautiful cradle for Timmy, in which he spent many hours while this loving neighbor tended to his needs, rocked him, and gently sang him to sleep. As Timmy grew older, Stella told him wonderful stories, played records for him, and showed him pictures of her as an actress. Stella cheered Timmy on as a Little League player, knitted sweaters for him, and provided him with enough money to invite a girl to his junior prom.

Today Timmy is happily married, with two young children of his own. He works as a high school gym teacher and during the basketball season as a coach. His recollections of his early experiences with his mother are primarily negative. He credits much of his day-to-day happiness and the success he experiences as an adult to the time he shared with Stella, with whom he still keeps in touch and to whom he never fails to send a card on Mother's Day.

Every child needs someone to love him and look after him. That person need not necessarily be the child's biological parent. If a family isolates a child from potentially beneficial and nurturing relationships, that child is likely to become a victim of maltreatment. The young person loses on two levels: he is denied both the possible prevention of maltreatment through an outsider's intervention and the healing effect of a kind person entering his life after he may have been mistreated.

Of course, everyone needs some privacy, and lack of social contact does not *cause* abuse or neglect. No one factor produces the same reaction in all people. Depending on their individual circumstances, some children may find themselves in a more vulnerable position than others. Still, isolation has been identified as a known factor that places the parent-child relationship in special jeopardy.

Wildlife studies have demonstrated that the same holds true for animals as for humans. When young gorilla mothers were separated from other gorillas and kept only with their offspring, these mothers neglected and abused their babies. After being brought back into the ape community, the mother gorillas once again exhibited healthy nurturing behavior toward their young. It seems that animals as well as humans need social contact in order to develop healthy patterns of behavior toward their young.

Social isolation and stressful conditions that lead to frustration and tension in the parent are factors that have been seen to increase the possibility of maltreatment. There are instances in which the parent may be willing to seek help from the community at large but, unfortunately, may find that no assistance is available. In fact, the community within which a child grows up can also have a bearing on his overall treatment. As the child grows and matures, his contacts with the larger world outside of his home broaden. Individuals other than his parents, as well as social agencies and organizations such as schools, after-school programs, churches, and clubs, will come to have an influence on his life. Where his environment is supportive and enriching, healthy development and creative functioning can occur. Where the environment is hostile, not protective of his needs, and depriving to the child, the resulting stress can damage normal growth and functioning.

Severe economic deprivation or poverty can also have an extremely damaging effect on the treatment the child may receive. Poor people often have fewer personal resources to draw upon and, therefore, their need for social resources and strong community agencies and support is great. If a child grows up in a neighborhood where nearly everybody is extremely poor, he may have a difficult time finding the sources he needs for enriched development. When the level of stress and distress within the community reaches an apex as well, there may be few available persons with spare time, love, or generosity to offer to a growing child.

Still another factor that often proves to be inherent in cases of child abuse is when the child himself actually serves as a stimulus for the abuse and victimization. Some children prove to be especially difficult for some people to parent. This is usually not the fault of the child, but is nonetheless an unavoidable aspect of his individuality. For example, a child who appears to be overly active, or unresponsive to loving gestures from his parent, may unintentionally provoke the wrath of the parent. If the parent has difficulty sympathizing as well as identifying with his offspring, the potential for abuse is greater. The child's resemblance to a disliked or resented person, or even the caretaker's jealousy of the child's relationship with another adult have been cited as factors that may provoke maltreatment from an adult who is prone to abusive behavior.

Parents do not own their children. They tend to them in trust for the rest of society. To maximize healthy growth and development, all children should grow up surrounded by social relationships which are personal, continuous, and enduring.

Psychological
Abuse

Many authorities on child development regard psychological abuse as the very center of the overall issue of maltreatment. When a child is abused psychologically, he is taught a false view of reality. He learns to see the world as a place where the significant people in his life are dominated by negative feelings and self-destructive patterns of behavior. The very people who are entrusted with the responsibility of teaching him to interact with others are themselves often incapable of relating to others as well as to him.

It is difficult to come up with a complete definition of what actually constitutes psychological abuse. Here we are dealing with a concept rather than a tangible, concrete pattern of behavior that can clearly be discerned or delineated. However, most authorities on child abuse agree that afflicting any of the behaviors listed below upon a child constitutes emotional or psychological abuse.

Humiliating the child
Using the child as a scapegoat
Calling the child names
Rejecting the child
Burdening the child with excessive responsibility
Forcing the child to attempt to conform to unrealistic expectations or unreasonable demands.

Research over the years has shown that parental rejection has a universally deleterious effect on children. Rejection by the parent leads to hostility, aggression, dependency, emotional instability, a low sense of self-esteem and self-worth, and a generally negative view of the world. These traits are also frequently seen in adults who were rejected as children. In studies in which mothers gazed down at their infants in their cribs but remained facially unresponsive (not smiling, laughing, or showing any change of expression), the infants responded with intense weariness and eventual withdrawal. Maternal rejection at even this early stage can be devastating.

After an infant is born, his helplessness and his responsiveness to those who care for him will usually help to captivate his caretakers and strengthen the emotional bond between him and his parents. Newborn babies are physiologically geared for social interaction. They prefer human faces to other objects and respond positively to the sound of voices. They enjoy and need touch, and bask in the arms of people who stroke and snuggle them.

Psychological or emotional abuse may be any behavior on the part of the parent or caretaker that entails the willful destruction of or serious damage to a child's growing competence. Usually an overall sense of personal competence and adequate development in a child is interpreted as including the following elements:

Communication skills: The child must be able to comprehend as well as transmit to others his thoughts and feelings verbally as well as with gestures.
Patience: The child must develop the ability to express his immediate feelings and emotions in a socially acceptable manner.

Realistic Goal Setting: The child must learn to recognize and set realistic challenges for himself.

Assurance—Self-Worth: The child must develop a basic sense of confidence and grow to feel secure about handling the ups and downs of everyday life.

Parents who psychologically abuse their children generally tend to ignore positive, healthy behavior exhibited by the child, and instead usually concentrate on the child's faults, often emphasizing even the child's minor unpleasant or "incorrect" actions. A loving parent who is actively involved with his offspring and maintains a healthy attitude toward life will be more likely to produce a child who enjoys a strong sense of self-worth and high self-esteem.

Every child has the right to decent care from his parents or caretakers. This means being cared for by someone who does not inflict his or her own needs on the child at the child's expense. It means having a parent who will not reject an infant's smiles, a toddler's curiosity in exploring his environment, or a school child's desire to make new friends and feel accepted by others.

4

Adolescent Abuse: A Unique Type of Maltreatment

The physical or emotional abuse of teenagers is a different phenomenon from the maltreatment of young children. The very fact that the victim himself is an adolescent or young adult makes it so.

A teenager's mental abilities and emotional makeup are likely to be more advanced than those of a young child. An adolescent will tend to reason much more like an adult than a child, and as a result the interaction between parent and offspring becomes considerably more complex. The adolescent's physical power and prowess are significantly greater than those of the young child. If an adolescent is assaulted by his parent, he may have the capacity to strike back with a forceful blow.

In addition, the adolescent has many more resources available to him that may influence parental conflicts in both positive and negative ways. For example, the adolescent has been around other families and adults. By this time he has some idea of what he does or does not deserve and what society at large deems appropriate behavior on his part and on the part of his parents. At this stage of his development, he is capable of bringing such comparisons into the conflict with his parent.

Many teenagers also become sophisicated enough to know what behavior on their part will trigger violent or aggressive behavior in their parent. These triggers can be pulled manipulatively by the teenager at significant times to embarrass either the parent or himself. Such actions only tend to intensify an already difficult, explosive family situation, but they take place nevertheless.

Adolescents have a substantially broader range of relationships than children do with people outside of the home. This plays a significant role in their lives. They may form close bonds with friends, teachers, aunts or uncles, employers, or other members of the community. Such relationships may tend to incite insecurity or jealousy in parents as they realize they are no longer the only important adult in their child's life. The normal development of boy-girl relationships during the teen years has been known to be particularly inflammatory to some parents because of the insinuation of possible sexual relations.

These new factors common to adolescence put stress on old family boundaries and methods of dealing with each other. Some parental behavior that was appropriate during their children's childhood is no longer appropriate during adolescence and may eventually explode into abusive situations. Spanking a three-year-old has a different psychological implication than trying to spank a sixteen-year-old. The same degree of intimacy and physical contact deemed affectionate behavior with a toddler may carry sexual implications when dealing with a young person past puberty. It is necessary for a parent or caretaker to oversee practically every aspect of a two-year-old's life, yet the same authoritarian approach in raising a teenager may signal overinvolvement of the parent.

Approximately half of the adolescents abused today were also abused as children. These young people simply continue to be the victims of their parent's inability to cope adequately with the role of caretaker. The other side of the statistic reflects the vast numbers of adolescents who were abused for the first time as teenagers. In both instances, power is generally the basic issue underlying adolescent abuse. In our society, children have very little power over their own lives. However, adolescence brings the young individual a new sense of power as he becomes aware of his increased ability to perceive, act, and engage in arguments.

Many teenagers deliberately challenge parental authority. Some parents treat their child's assertive behavior as a challenge to their position.

A teenager in an abusive situation is faced with a serious dilemma. It has been shown that even severely abused adolescents often experience anxiety and guilt when they are finally separated from their tormentors. They have been told so often that they are worthless that many come to believe their powerful parent's distorted view of life and of the adolescent's own merit. At times, abused teenagers' personal sense of worth and value has been so diminished that they may even come to believe their abuser's justifications for abusing them. They may wrongly feel that they are receiving just or necessary punishment for their actions.

Joannie, a sixteen-year-old abuse victim, had lived alone with her father for the two years since her parents' divorce. The young girl's plight came to the attention of the authorities when a neighbor—in an anonymous phone call—described Joannie's home situation to the Bureau of Child Welfare.

Joannie's home was a one-bedroom apartment that had come to look and smell like a garbage heap. Although the apartment had been parcelled off by her father so that he slept in the bedroom and Joannie spent most of her time in the living area, he used their living-room floor as if it were a hamper for his dirty clothes. At times, when Joannie attempted to either hang up or wash her father's clothing, he beat her severely, accusing her of going through his pants to steal his money. When she left her father's things where he had dropped them, he would beat her as punishment for not cleaning up, usually calling her lazy, sloppy, and useless.

At times, the apartment reeked of a foul odor, because when Joannie's father had had too much to drink, he would often vomit in bed and sometimes not change the sheets for weeks. Since he had told Joannie that if he ever caught her sneaking around in the bedroom he would kill her, she dared not venture into that forbidden territory.

In some ways Joannie might be considered more fortunate than most abused teens, because, although Joannie had not seen or heard from her mother in two years, after her predicament became known she was offered a viable opportunity for change. The authorities contacted Joannie's nearest relative, her mother's sister, Janet.

Joannie's Aunt Janet was a happily married woman in her forties who lived in a spacious, comfortable home. Unable to have children of her own, Joannie's Aunt Janet stressed that she would cherish having a young girl in her home to raise. Joannie's aunt and uncle offered to legally adopt her and give her the best life they were capable of providing.

A family-court judge put the final decision in Joannie's own hands. Her initial decision was to remain with her father. She explained that she had grown up in the apartment and that she felt anxious about leaving the only home she had ever known. She also expressed a great deal of apprehension about leaving her father, explaining that her mother had abandoned her when her parents divorced, and now she felt that if she moved away she might lose the only parent she had left.

After being encouraged by a social worker to give her aunt's offer a try, Joannie consented to spend a week at her aunt and uncle's home. The time she spent with her relatives seemed like something out of a Hollywood movie for Joannie, yet at the end of the week she chose to return to her father despite her aunt and uncle's pleas for her to remain with them permanently.

Joannie later told the social worker that she felt uncomfortable with all the comforts her Aunt Janet wished to give her. She felt guilty over leaving her father in their hovel of an apartment while she lived in a beautiful home, even though it was her father's living habits that had largely created the present condition of their apartment. She also expressed fear that if she went to live with her relatives, her father might disown her. At one point she told the social worker that she didn't feel right taking what her relatives offered her because "a piece of junk like me doesn't deserve to live that way."

Because many abused adolescents have never lived

away from home, they are often dependent on the person who is abusing them and are unable to conceive of a successful life away on their own. Fear of separation from the parental figure can actually paralyze whatever inner resources the victim might have, and may lead him to deny his own hurt even to himself. If the thought of breaking away is too frightening, the victim may choose to minimize his own maltreatment rather than report it to the authorities.

Society tends to be highly sympathetic to very young abused children, but is not always as universally supportive of teenagers who have endured maltreatment. At times these young people are stereotyped as "behavior-problem teens" who provoked uncontrollable rage in their parents. Some people might even feel that such a teenager "got what was coming to him."

It is also often presumed that teenagers have the resources to leave their homes if they choose to do so. They are not regarded in the same way as an infant who has been beaten while lying innocently and helplessly in his crib. Actually, most adolescents are both financially and emotionally completely dependent on their caretakers. When an abused teenager, like an abused wife, does not take advantage of the assistance of outside agencies, he is often unfairly viewed as an integral part of the problem. Altering the family situation may take the form of counseling, foster care, institutionalization, or a semi-independent living arrangement.

The character of a parent who abuses his adolescent offspring for the first time differs somewhat from the parent guilty of abusing a young child. Studies have shown that parents who first became abusive during their offspring's adolescence are usually older than parents who abuse younger children.

While abuse of infants and young children appears to be most heavily concentrated among single parents and poor people, reported instances of adolescent abuse seem to be spread more evenly throughout the general population of our society. Researchers warn of the danger of stereotyping any one group of people into this role.

Very young children are more likely to be the victims of extremely severe abuse than are older children. Over 40 percent of reported cases of maltreatment of infants involved severe abuse, while this was true of only 3 percent of the cases involving adolescents. Abuse of teenagers is much more likely to involve psychological patterns of maltreatment rather than life-threatening physical assault.

The experience of being abused varies markedly according to each individual situation and set of circumstances. In addition, the effect of abuse on the victim will be different for individuals who first came to know maltreatment as teenagers than for those young people who were abused throughout their childhoods.

At times the level of conflict within a family may erupt into adolescent abuse over a particular issue or because the adolescent himself has introduced some new elements into the family relationship. This happens most frequently in families in which the young person has been overindulged or spoiled by his parents. A parent who has been overly involved in his child's development and life will have a difficult time letting go when the child is ready to expand his own sense of independence. This type of caretaker demands excessive dependency and complete compliance from the teenager. He expects his child to belong to him totally in mind and spirit in return for all the trips, presents, treats, etc., which he has showered on him throughout the years.

Such feelings can grow into frustration, resistance, anger, and rage, as the youth matures and begins to act more like an adult. The normal strivings of a teenager to define his sense of indentity and self may be enough to enrage the parent. In some instances, this may lead to inappropriate and abusive behavior as a means of trying to control him.

Another common type of abuse is linked to adolescence only by coincidence. In these instances, maltreatment began in infancy or childhood and simply continued during the teen years. The abuse inflicted on the child has nothing to do with the child's age or development into a young adult. It may seem unbelievable that abuse to any individual might be allowed to continue from childhood through adolescence without an outside agency interceding, but it happens very often. This is particularly true in situations where the abuse does not dramatically escalate at any given point, but continues at about the same level throughout the child's residence in the home.

Still another type of abuse against young people

erupts when previously mild or moderate forms of corporal punishment escalate into abusive behavior. A person who was spanked as a child might find that now that he is an adolescent, his parent has taken to beating him with a strap. This is common among parents who find it necessary to severely restrict their offspring's behavior in order to feel that they are still firmly in charge. Threatened by their teenager's increasing size, strength, and independence, these adults apply additional force in the name of discipline.

In general, the later the abuse is initiated in an individual's life, the more likely it is that he will be less damaged, because he has already had a number of healthy developmental years to fall back on.

In the normal developmental scheme, adolescence is a period for changing, growing, and seeking new forms of freedom and independence. The adolescent experiences biological, intellectual, and social changes that affect his life. It is a time when a person will try on adult roles and test how it feels to assert himself in many new and different ways. The disruption in family roles brought about by this testing in the home can often serve to ignite the sparks of maltreatment.

The adolescent years mark a milestone in physical and sexual development for most human beings. Puberty signals the maturation of the sexual organs as well as such secondary sex characteristics as facial hair and a lower-pitched voice in boys and breast development and a widening of the pelvis in girls. The hormones that accompany such physical changes may also be responsible for mood fluctuations in many people. Such biological changes often go hand in hand with an increased interest in members of the opposite sex, as well as the initiation of dating. Other aspects of life common to the adolescent years, such as curfews, dating activities, friends, and the choice of dating partners, are all volatile issues that may affect relationships within the family.

The concept of teenage sexuality in any form can be extremely disturbing to many parents. Parents are forced to trust their teenagers to uphold the moral values they have attempted to instill in them throughout their developmental years. When dealing with emotional issues such as chastity, trust, and a teenager's newly felt need to assert himself, emotions often flare—and in many cases abusive behavior may come into play.

Another change in the teenager with which a parent must learn to cope is the intellectual development and related personality changes that usually accompany adolescence. The teen years bring an increased ability to ponder and deal with hypothetical problems. Adolescents learn to think abstractly about academic subjects as well as their own feelings, their parents, and their relationship to others. Teenagers, unlike children, are often no longer willing to automatically accept another person's point of view. Usually, they are able to come up with an evaluation of matters on their own. At this point of their lives, they can often more clearly discern their parents' true motivation in various situations.

While this ability may enable the teenager to make a more in-depth analysis of his school studies, it also means that his parents will perhaps for the first time in their lives have to deal with a young person in their home who can think and reason independently of their guidance. Many abusive parents find, to their distaste, that they are no longer able to mold their offspring's thinking to the extent that they might wish to.

Perhaps one of the most striking changes that accompanies adolescence occurs in the realm of social development. At this stage of their lives, many teenagers may appear to be overly concerned with evaluation and acceptance by their friends or peer group. This new emphasis is actually an attempt by adolescents to separate from their parents and establish an identity of their own.

A teenager's circle of friends may greatly influence the way he dresses, what he eats, with whom he socializes, and how he spends his time both in and out of school. While at one time this young person might have tried to please his parents, now his efforts might be turned much more toward winning the approval of his friends. At times, the parents of a teenager may come to miss the esteem their child once held for them and may feel somewhat displaced by their teenager's set of friends.

In many instances, the abusive parent may feel that he is in competition with the adolescent's friends. Parents who are overly involved with their child may believe that their teenager's style of dress or his general appearance reflects their success or failure as caretakers. They may feel unjustifiably that they must control their adolescent's life more rigidly, even though it may be nearly impossible to closely monitor a teenager's activities away from home. The end result may be highly charged disciplinary sessions that can lead to abuse.

A healthy parent must learn to adapt to the adolescent's new growth and strivings. It is best for everyone concerned that parents be able to listen to their young, discuss issues that affect the entire family, and explain the reasoning behind certain rules or limitations. Living in a healthy, productive environment with a teenager requires listening and communication skills.

Outside forces can bring further pressures to bear upon families with adolescents. The adolescent occupies a difficult role in our society. Being somewhere between child and adult, adolescents face limitations and restrictions in almost every area of their lives. In earlier times when people died at a significantly younger age, positions of respect and responsibility were often accorded to young people. (In fact, many of the early settlers coming to the New World were actually teenagers.) The frustration of not being taken seriously often contributes to tense family interactions.

Unfortunately, our society offers very few tangible guidelines that help to define clearly the adolescent's ascent to adulthood. Although there are legal age limitations set on the right to vote, drive a car, or drink alcoholic beverages, it is often difficult for a parent to accurately gauge at what point his offspring is ready to take on new responsibilities. The differing views between parent and teenager regarding what is suitable behavior for an adolescent often explode into bitter disputes that may lead to abuse.

The tensions discussed in this chapter cannot of themselves turn a healthy, well-functioning parent into an abusive caretaker. Many families are able to successfully cope with and overcome the stresses adolescence bring. In times of severe stress, some families even become more closely knit, through resolving their difficulties together.

More often than not, however, this is not the case. Parents who are particularly vulnerable, who might already have been experiencing difficulty in their role as caretakers, may react to new, additional pressures by resorting to violent outbursts. Parents who are especially susceptible to eventually maltreating their children are those who are experiencing low self-esteem, marital difficulties, poor communication between family members, and an excessive need or desire to control.

Lynn's Story

(These are the taped and transcribed words of an abused adolescent girl)

My mother died on my thirteenth birthday. I've always thought that it was kind of strange. I mean her leaving the world on the anniversary of the same day I entered it. My father said that he had rushed to the hospital to see my mother for the last time as soon as they had called him at work to relay the bad news. But he was too late. By the time he arrived, my mom's body had been placed in a large plastic bag and was resting on a slab to be taken down to the morgue. I never saw the bag, but my father said that it was light blue in color, and that you could see the outline of my mom's limbs underneath the thin plastic. Just the thought of my mother being stuffed into what seemed to me to be like a giant blue baggie created an image in my mind that I haven't been able to dismiss from my consciousness. It's all just too horrible to try to deal with.

I didn't have too happy a thirteenth birthday, as you can imagine, and with my mother gone I didn't expect to have too happy a life from then on. My mother had been carrying on her personal battle with cancer for just about the past year and a half. That was in addition to the continuous battle that she waged ever since I can remember to try to get my father to keep his hands off her and me and my older sister Beth.

According to my father, nothing any of us did was ever good enough. He often beat my mother with little or no provocation, and after Beth entered high school, he really started hitting her hard too. Once a couple of months ago, he knocked my sister into a corner in our room and began punching her face on both sides, first the right side and then the left. He wouldn't stop until Beth had collapsed. Then as she lay there unconscious on the floor, he gave her a good hard kick in the stomach. That night I was really afraid that he had finally killed Beth. I've always thought that it was a miracle that she survived. When I asked him why he did it, he said that it was to teach my sister a lesson. But I still didn't understand what Beth had done wrong to begin with.

Of course deep inside, I knew that Beth hadn't done anything wrong. Real transgressions were not necessary to provoke my dad's rage. He was able to imagine and magnify wrongdoings at whim. Naturally, he set himself up as the judge as well as the executor of whatever punishments he determined that we deserved. You only had to have the wrong expression on your face, or put too much butter on his toast, to merit a beating that you would not soon forget.

I remember how when I was in the tenth grade the dance teacher had selected me to dance the lead in a tap dance number in our class's recital. I felt thrilled by the very thought of it. I loved to dance and had practiced so hard throughout all of this year as well as last. I had often been complimented on my ability by my classmates, but I never allowed myself to believe that I was really any good. But this kind of recognition from Miss Brady, our dance instructor, made my heart leap.

I wanted to be good, very good—maybe even outstanding. And I wanted everyone to see me shining, perhaps most especially my dad. Even though my father usually alternated between showing me affection and cruelty, I still never gave up hoping to win him over. I longed for him to think that I was a good dancer, to believe that I was beautiful rather than clumsy, and to be proud that I had been chosen to dance the lead in our recital.

But, unfortunately, things didn't go as I had wished. When I proudly told him about my being chosen to dance the lead and promised him a front row seat if he came to the program, he immediately became incensed at my having approached him at all. He stated that I was a no-good burden who was always nagging him to go to this place or to that place. And then he grabbed one of my tap shoes, which I had been holding, out of my hand and started hitting me across the face with it. I tried to run from him, but he soon overtook me, pinned me down on the bed, and continued beating my face with the shoe. The metal tap on the heel ripped my skin and I had to have eleven stiches. My whole face was swollen and discolored for what seemed like a long time.

I was ashamed to go to school for the next two weeks. I just couldn't face having any of the kids see me looking like that. I lost my part in the dance recital, but now I didn't care. Nothing seemed to matter any more. I really didn't think I'd be able to go on like this much longer. I began to wish that I had been the one put in the blue plastic bag instead of my mother.

Portrait of the Victim: The Effects of Abuse

I came home about a half an hour later than I was supposed to on Saturday night. He didn't give me a chance to explain . . . he just came at me with a razor strap. He hit me hard that night, real hard. He just wouldn't stop beating on me. His strap left welts on my arms, neck, back, and legs. The next day it was hard for me to walk, or to even stand, for that matter. But I know that he was right. My father wouldn't have beat me like that if I hadn't been bad. He would have never done it if everything hadn't been my fault.

Jennie at age 15

Children are born without any inherent value scheme. They have no way of judging their own worth. People learn what is right or wrong, as well as what is appropriate or inappropriate behavior, from what their parents teach them as children.

Abuse and neglect can have a devastating effect on how a young person comes to view himself and the world around him. Abuse, over a long period throughout a person's childhood, has a significantly more harmful effect than does abuse begun for the first time during adolescence. Studies have shown that teenagers who have been abused since early childhood may be damaged emotionally in a variety of ways.

For an adolescent to become a healthy, well-functioning adult, he must acquire a sense of competence and feel secure about his ability to have an effect on his environment. He needs a positive sense of family or parents with which to identify and feel as if he belongs. For the young person's optimal development and psychological adjustment, parents should allow their teenager to have some say in the decision-making process. Properly effective parents must be able to gradually expand their teenager's realm of responsibility so that he comes to feel that he possesses some power within the family setting as well as the outside world.

Children and adolescents are extremely adaptable beings; they can survive within a wide range of situations. Youths living in hostile-abusive environments learn to adjust, in one way or another, to painful experiences. Unfortunately, over the course of time, unhealthy environments damage an individual's development.

One danger is that children learn to become successful or unsuccessful adults by identifying with and imitating those who take care of them. Children become like their parents because of the emotional bonds between them as well as the fact that their early formative years are spent with their parents. It is natural for children to copy the people who matter to them. Young people absorb whatever atmosphere they are exposed to, whether it is a warm and loving one or a distorted, violent one.

When a child identifies with an aggressive parent, he incorporates the hostility surrounding him into his own behavior. Through abuse and maltreatment, a parent is using his behavior to say the child isn't worth very much. A young child who has known only severe punishment and no affection from his caretakers will eventually come to believe that he is bad and deserves this type of treatment.

As one young victim expressed it: "Once while my father was beating me, he took a glass ashtray off the coffee table and flung it right at my face. I was afraid that I might lose my left eye. My whole face felt sore for weeks. But I don't hold it against him. After all, he's my father, isn't he?" This young person lacked any awareness that no human being merits this type of treatment under any circumstances.

Studies have shown that children with high self-esteem are better able to handle challenges, express creativity and inventive thinking, and deal with situations in a thorough, competent manner. A person with low self-esteem thinks poorly of himself and believes that he will fail. As a result of such thinking, the individual often will in fact fail. It is almost as if such a person's actions match his negative thinking and expectations. Children and adolescents with low self-esteem are more likely to display problem behavior in school and social settings, experience a high degree of anxiety, and exhibit destructive tendencies toward objects and people.

One of the greatest difficulties professionals face in treating abuse victims is the task of convincing such individuals that they are worthwhile, valuable human beings. Continual parental criticism not only causes misery at the given moment, but also serves to dampen the child's hopes and dreams for the future. In some instances, an overall climate of rejection for a prolonged period can have an even more damaging effect than one or two startlingly dramatic incidents during an individual's childhood.

Children suffering from low self-esteem experience a great deal of anxiety. Because young people who have been maltreated think so poorly of themselves, they often become overly dependent on the opinions and assurances of others. Believing that they are not capable of doing anything right, they may become unusually apprehensive about doing or saying the wrong thing around their friends. Having little or no self-confidence can cause a great deal of anxiety in social situations.

Sarah is perhaps an extreme example of a young victim of psychological abuse who had come to believe that she was worthless. At sixteen Sarah had spent the last decade or so of her life hearing constantly from both her stepfather and her mother that she was ugly, stupid, and clumsy. Sarah was actually none of the above, as most of her teachers and classmates told her, but she had been fed so much other, more destructive information over the years that it became, for her, reality. That's what she really believed.

Sarah felt that she had to work with extra diligence to maintain the relationships that come naturally to most people. She saved her allowance and the money she earned babysitting to buy her girlfriends and her boyfriend Jonathan small presents. In sports and games, she often gave up her turn to allow others to go ahead of her. When she went to the movies with her friends, she always took the seat behind the tall person.

Sarah claimed to be very much in love with her boyfriend Jonathan. However, her good feelings about

Jonathan were always mixed with a sense of anxiety. She never quite believed that someone as fabulous as Jonathan was hers, and she always feared he would leave her.

Sarah and Jonathan usually got along quite well. Yet one important area of contention existed between them. Sarah was a virgin and wished to remain one until she married. Because of Sarah's poor self-image, she was extremely afraid of doing anything that might be considered immoral. Jonathan had little tolerance for what he called Sarah's outmoded values. He told Sarah that they were in love, and that lovemaking was just an expression of their feelings for one another. What had the greatest impact on insecure Sarah was that Jonathan told her that if she didn't have sex with him, he'd leave her. Jonathan argued that it didn't make sense for them to abstain, since they were eventually going to be married.

Sarah finally gave in to Jonathan's sexual demands. Two weeks later, he left her. Jonathan told Sarah that it had nothing to do with him thinking any less of her for having gone to bed with him, but rather that now he realized that they were too young to make a serious commitment to one another and that he still wanted to date other girls. Whether or not Jonathan was telling the truth had nothing to do with the way his actions affected Sarah. She had always felt that she was worthless and now by leaving her Jonathan had unwittingly confirmed her feelings. Having had sex with him made Sarah feel more degraded than loved.

The last person Sarah talked to was her friend Lynn

on Saturday morning. She told Lynn that it didn't really matter that she was no longer a virgin, since she was sure that no one would ever want to marry her in any case. Lynn saw that Sarah was severely depressed and tried to cheer her up, but nothing she said seemed to help.

After Lynn left that afternoon, Sarah became extremely despondent. On Saturday night, while her mother and stepfather were out at the movies, Sarah jumped off the patio of their twentieth floor apartment. Sarah died immediately. She had left a note saying that she "didn't want to feel bad anymore."

Anxiety is also a factor in academic failure. Young people learn best when they are free of psychological pressures and can experience good feelings about themselves. It may seem ironic, but children and adolescents who do not do very well in school are often more critical of themselves than students who earn high marks. Self-criticism becomes the poor student's defense against an onslaught of criticism he may expect from others.

In addition, a young person's anxiety over his aggressive feelings can result in some form of violent expression of these feelings. People who are anxious about aggression often respond more aggressively than others to situations that may evoke such feelings.

Maltreatment tends to exaggerate a young person's uncertainty about himself and the world around him. Another unfortunate by-product of such abuse is lack of empathy in victims of maltreatment. The ability to empathize is the ability to place oneself in the circumstances of another and feel what that person would be feeling. The phrase "walk a mile in my shoes" perhaps best captures the meaning of empathy. The ability to identify with another person's feelings and responses fosters a humane and forgiving society. People behave more responsibly when they are aware of the effect their behavior will have on others.

An empathetic person is one who can be sympathetic and who at times will work hard in order to help another individual. The benefits of empathy, both to the person and to society at large, are numerous. It has been found that children who are empathetic score higher on academic tests. An empathetic child tends to be less hostile and aggressive in school and social situations. Many people believe that empathy is the very cornerstone of morality in our society.

Many abused young people lose their ability to empathize at an early age, and some never develop it at all. Since they were never shown empathy while they were growing up, they exhibit the same lack of empathy their parents demonstrated to them. Many teenagers who have been abused will respond to younger children in very much the same manner in which their parents responded to them. They cannot identify with the child's needs.

Along with feelings of low self-esteem and a lack of empathy, rejection is common among abused young people. Parental rejection can make a young person extremely dependent on his friends and other adults. Those who do not know love and acceptance in their early years may seek it ferociously for much of their lives. Their search for acceptance combined with their feelings of worthlessness may often prime such individuals to become targets for poor treatment from other abusive people they may encounter. These individuals do not perceive the treatment they receive as terrible—this is all they have ever known. In instances where they do realize that they are being treated poorly, they often still do not break away. They firmly believe that they do not deserve any better. Abuse is reminiscent of their past, and they feel deserving of mistreatment. Abusive treatment may become the distinctive characteristic of the majority of their social relationships and interactions.

Such people are extremely vulnerable to hurt and rejection from others in their lives and may find it extremely difficult to abandon the victim role. Studies have shown that adolescents whose parents were either extremely lenient and permissive or strict and authoritarian tend to be overly concerned with conformity and acceptance from their friends. Some of these teens seem almost slavish in their desire to please. It may seem ironic that two such extremely different home environments would tend to produce the same reaction in young people. But neither method of parenting afforded the young person what was needed for him to become an independent, well-functioning, separate individual.

The type of social and behavioral problems exhibited by mistreated youths often tends to reflect the nature of the abuse they underwent. A teenager who is the victim of neglect and has grown up feeling alone and isolated will not necessarily show the same effects as a young person who was repeatedly raped by a parent.

Parents who are overly controlling may especially inflict damage on their offspring. Every young person needs a certain amount of freedom and space within which to grow up. Parents who are extremely restrictive and tend to limit their child's growth and opportunities for new experiences may often produce dependent children.

Clinical studies have also shown that children brought up in an overly controlled environment tend to become involved in quarrels more often, and are generally considered less popular among their peers, than other children. Youths who have been dealt severe punishment tend to be less affectionate, less verbal, and are often exceptionally submissive. Some researchers believe that the extreme submissiveness apparent in such young people may be the end result of ruthless domination.

Although a teenager who has been somewhat neglected and has lacked parental control, proper guidance, and discipline may become involved in some deviant antisocial behavior, statistics reveal that overly controlled youths fare far worse. Rigidly controlled young people often grow up to become extremely assaultive adults. Police records show that many such individuals have been guilty of committing homicide, assault and battery, and various other violent offenses. Outwardly, these people may appear extremely well controlled, but inside they feel alienated, repressed, and wrathful. Often when interviewed, the neighbors or coworkers of people who have committed murders, will describe the perpertrator as "quiet" or "someone who kept to himself." Yet that person was very much like a human powder keg, ready to blow up without warning.

For many abused youths, the major challenge of their lives becomes finding ways to escape the feelings of pain and humiliation that so often characterize their daily existence. Some have turned to drugs or alcohol, others have even attempted suicide. Numerous studies have borne out a clear connection between damaged family relationships and the misuse of drugs among adolescents.

Desperately unhappy children and young adults who see only very limited alternatives or none at all for a brighter future may contemplate taking their own lives. It has been found that children who have succeeded in their suicide attempts have often been driven to this drastic solution out of abuse, neglect, or grief. Suicide is seen by these young people as the only means by which to escape the pervasive pain that dominates their lives.

Adolescents who commit suicide usually have an extensive history of family problems that began in their childhood. Many of them come from homes that are characterized by rage, inconsistent parental expectations, parental rejection, and extreme punishment. Parental alcoholism is another factor often associated with suicidal adolescents.

At times, a suicide attempt may be a disguised cry for

help. It may be the only way of telling his parents as well as others in the child's life that something is seriously wrong with the way things are going.

Even if the young person's life is saved, his plea for change may go unheard and unacknowledged. The youth's drastic attempt to call attention to the family situation and to rectify the distorted parent-child relationship may be unsuccessful. The child may go on living, but as unhappily as before.

In numerous studies, the major difference found between maltreated youths who attempted suicide and those who did not was that while neither group was able to relate well to their parents, the young people who did not attempt to kill themselves had managed to maintain some relatively meaningful contacts with friends of their own age as well as with adults outside the home. Unfortunately, many victims of abuse do not develop adequate social skills. Without friends they come to feel extremely isolated and cut off from others. In times of severe distress, they may believe that there is no one to whom they can turn, and suicide may appear to be the only way out.

Children and adolescents who try to die feel an extreme sense of hopelessness. They feel helpless and abandoned in intolerable situations, and suicide is the alternative they've turned to after everything else has failed.

Another effect of abuse often seen in varying degrees in both children and adolescents is deviant or delinquent behavior. Abused youths often grow up with psychological problems that make it difficult for them to cope in normal society. Such individuals often experience difficulty dealing with the restrictions or constraints of school or any outside environment. In many instances, such young people have been labeled troubled, at risk, antisocial, or wayward. Many will skip days at school or even drop out altogether, indulge in drugs or alcohol, and engage in inappropriate sexual behavior. Such behavior not only adds to the misery they are experiencing in their present lives, but jeopardizes their future as well. Substance abuse can be addictive and personally destructive, just as dropping out of school may permanently relegate an individual to a low-paying, uninspiring job. The results of sexual promiscuity may be an undesired pregnancy, venereal disease, and an even further damaged sense of self-esteem.

Studies have shown that there is a correlation between deliquent behavior in youth and the eventual emergence of an antisocial adult personality. Such a person may frequently become involved in criminal activity. Typical kinds of behavior found to be accurate predictors of an antisocial personality were theft, associating with other delinquent youths, violating curfews excessively, running away, fighting, difficulty in following rules at school, lying without cause, recklessness, and being unable to express love or show guilt or remorse. Exhibiting any one or more of these actions doesn't necessarily mean that the youth will become an antisocial adult. However, it has been shown that the greater the number of these traits exhibited during childhood or adolescence, the more likely it is that the person will experience a troublesome adulthood.

There is a strong link between juvenile delinquency and the maltreatment of youth. Neglect plays a part in all of this as well. An interesting finding of a recent study was that children who believed that their parents were not aware of their whereabouts were considerably more likely to become involved in delinquent acts. A child who does not feel firmly bonded to his parents will be less likely to develop a strong sense of conscience and morality.

Bert, a fourteen year-old abuse victim, was put on a year's probation after a mild run-in with the law. As a stipulation of his probation, Bert was required to go for both individual and family therapy. Early in their sessions together, Bert described to the counselor how he had been a victim of psychological and physical abuse since his early childhood.

Bert's parents had used their child as a scapegoat for their own rage and feelings of personal inadequacy ever since he could remember. If Bert's father had had a difficult day at his office, when he came home in the evening, he would often call his four-year-old son a "yellow-bellied coward" and knock the boy to the ground. It was a bizarre predicament for Bert, totally unrelated to his own behavior and completely out of his control. Through family counseling it was revealed later that Bert's father had felt that in certain situations he had lacked the courage and initiative to speak up to his own supervisor at work. At these times he imagined himself to be more powerful by projecting his own feelings of weakness onto his son and then by punishing the boy.

Bert had fared little better under his mother's care. If his mother didn't like the way her hair looked that day or if she had put on a few pounds, she was capable of flying into a rage and beating her young son severely with a strap or belt. Often she would scream at the boy and humiliate him publicly. At least two or three times a week she told Bert that she had been cursed because abortions were not legal when she was pregnant and now she was forced to raise him.

Without ever really being fully aware of it, Bert soon came to feel that his parents expected him to misbehave. As a result, he began to live up to their expectations. If Bert did something well, his achievement was quickly glossed over. He was severely punished for any wrongdoings, and it soon became apparent that this was the only time he received his parents' attention at all.

Bert began to exhibit problem behavior at school. He became involved in frequent playground fights and was often truant. By the time Bert reached his early teens he had become involved with drugs, vandalized public property, and had been picked up by the police for shoplifting.

Bert's counselor described Bert's actions as growing out of the young boy's rage at his mistreatment, besides being a futile attempt on Bert's part to capture his parents' attention and concern. Bert had never won praise for good behavior. Now he felt certain that his parents didn't want him around to disrupt their lives with his presence. Acting within the limits of the law was not going to guarantee Bert a happy home life, and he hurt inside enough to want to lash out at someone or something.

Agressive children are often found to be the offspring of parents who have dealt with them in an aggressive manner. Often, overly aggressive children have been treated with hostility or were rejected, and are relatively unaccustomed to receiving warmth and support. Some researchers have characterized abusive fathers of chronic delinquents as being cruel, self-centered, and often absent from the home. Abusive mothers were found to be neglectful, incompetent, and rejecting.

Researchers have also found that young male victims of maltreatment tend to become aggressive, while female victims are more likely to turn to self-destructive responses. This may be reflective of living in a culture that still strongly frowns on any expression of aggressiveness in females. Maltreated boys will often express their rage over being abused in an aggressive, sometimes assaultive manner, such as drinking, brawling, or reckless driving, while young girls are more likely to take the same feelings of anger and hurt and turn them inward against themselves. Such self-destructive actions may take the form of running away from home, alcohol or drug abuse, defying curfews, sexual promiscuity, and similar acts.

It is interesting to note that in very recent years aggresssive delinquent acts committed by young women appear to be on the rise. As traditional roles become more relaxed, we may continue to see more of a shift in this direction. Still, regardless of the form taken by the young person's destructive response to maltreatment, the problem of her abuse within her home environment remains.

There appears to be a distinct correlation between the use of violence in the home under the guise of discipline and resulting aggressive delinquent acts on the part of young males. In one study, over 95 percent of the young delinquent boys involved had undergone extremely severe corporal punishment in their homes that had continued unabated for a number of years. Many of these boys had been whipped with belts or extension cords as well as smacked with heavy boards or brutally beaten with fists.

The devastating effects of the severe corporal abuse of children bear serious and dangerous consequences for all of society as well as for the youths themselves. There is a definite connection between abuse and homicide. An astonishing number of teenagers who have actually committed murder were severely physically abused during their childhood. In addition, a strikingly large number of infamous murders were committed by individuals who had been abused as children. Charles Manson, the cult leader responsible for the brutal murder of actress Sharon Tate and others, is one example.

On May 15, 1972, a young man named Arthur Bremer attempted to assassinate Governor George Wallace of Alabama by shooting him. Fortunately, the governor lived. The recordings of court procedures as well as files from several of the social agencies to which Bremer had been known reflected an early childhood background of neglect and violence.

On June 6, 1968, Sirhan B. Sirhan assassinated Robert Kennedy. After American journalists traced the origins of Sirhan's background and childhood in Palestine, it was revealed through neighbors' testimony that Sirhan's father frequently brutally beat all of his children.

James Earl Ray, the eldest of nine children, shot and killed Dr. Martin Luther King, Jr., on April 4, 1968. Many of the Ray children spent portions of their childhoods in various foster homes. Remaining in the Ray home itself often meant surviving a severe degree of poverty and neglect.

Lee Harvey Oswald, who shot and killed John F. Kennedy in Dallas, Texas, on November 22, 1963, was also the victim of a pained and troubled childhood. In elementary school he was diagnosed early as being emotionally disturbed. His problem behavior led to his being admitted to a special training institution for youths, but Lee Harvey Oswald was never to become smoothly integrated into the mainstream of our society.

The effects of maltreatment are considerably more far-reaching than one might initially realize. Abuse not only destroys the child victim, but jeopardizes the foundation of a humane society.

Sexual
Abuse

Children are born into this world totally dependent on their parents or other caretakers for their survival and welfare. Parents are expected to provide unconditional care, protection, and emotional support to their children. Although there may be numerous rewards inherent in parenting, a child can never be justifiably expected to care for his parent in return. A normal healthy parent cannot realistically demand that his child fulfill his own personal needs for food, clothing, shelter, or sex. Whenever a parent tries to deny his child the right to remain a child, and compels the youngster to act as a partner, an exploitative situation comes into being. That child becomes the victim of sexual abuse.

When a parent coerces a child into a sexual encounter of any type, the protective bond between them is broken. The child is forced, through the use of his body, to pay for the normal care and affection, which should be freely given. It doesn't matter whether the actual sexual interchanges are brutal or pleasurable; the effect on the child's normal emotional and sexual development is always destructive.

Female children are more often subject to sexual assault than young boys. In most cases the aggressors are not strangers, but rather neighbors, family friends, uncles, stepfathers, and fathers. Sexual exploitation by a known and trusted adult has unfortunately become a reality in the lives of countless young girls.

Incest between mothers and sons is not a very common occurrence. Most reported cases reveal a marked social deviance or severe psychopathology involving the mother, the son, or both. A large number of mother-son incest incidents involve the rape of the mother by an adolescent boy. When a young boy is molested by a parent, the aggressor is as likely to be his father as his mother. In fact, the vast majority of sexual contacts between boys and adults are homosexual.

Sexual encounters between parents and children always involve coercion on some level by the parent. The adult holds the position of power within the family structure. There is no way that a child could realistically be in control or genuinely exercise free choice.

Children are captives within the family situation. They are likely to take their parent's threats seriously. Afraid of being either abandoned or rejected by their caretakers, the children may feel compelled to go along with the adult's demands. They often obey even though such actions make them feel guilty, frightened, or ashamed of their own bodies. Many proceed with whatever is required of them, even though they may feel that they'd rather die. Out of fear and dependency, most children feel forced to swallow their own objections and obey their parents.

The overpowering feeling of coercion, without regard for the child's own sense of self, may be part of the reason that, as adults, former sexual-abuse victims often recall their incestuous experiences as being overwhelmingly negative. The age difference between the adult and the child and the degree of force employed in the interchange have also been isolated as factors to take into account in evaluating how the experience is remembered.

Child victims of sexual abuse often sustain damage

that lasts many years. This has been found to be especially true in instances where force was employed, where the incestuous relationship was sustained over a long period, or when the sexual aggressor was a close member of the family unit.

Researchers have found that many women with a childhood history of sexual abuse suffer from a sense of low self-esteem as adults. These women often experience sexual difficulties in adulthood. Some described themselves as frigid and said that topics of a sexual nature didn't interest them. Their emotional reactions were often extremely intense, and they quickly turned away from any sexual subject.

Other women who had been sexually abused as children had almost an opposite reaction. Instead of describing themselves as frigid, these women stated that they were promiscuous by their own standards. The second group of women complained that as adults they found that they had experienced difficulty in maintaining long-term relationships with members of the opposite sex. Many felt compelled to have numerous sexual partners, and some said they felt the only way to win a man's love was to seduce him.

The vast majority of women who were sexually abused as children appeared to have adopted a victim role as adults. Many of these women had been adolescent runaways, battered wives, or at some time had become involved in prostitution. The women complained of feeling isolated and cut off from others. They said they mistrusted men and exhibited a marked tendency to repeat their history of becoming involved in abusive love relationships. Childhood victims of sexual abuse generally had a great deal of difficulty in attaining a firm feeling of self-respect and a positive sexual identity. Never having learned to protect themselves, these women often appeared to be easy targets for men who wish to exploit them.

Many former incest victims feel that they've been forced to live with feelings of depression and loneliness throughout their lives. It is difficult for them to develop trust in intimate relationships, as they believe that they were betrayed by both their parents—a father who sexually abused them and a mother who allowed it to happen.

Since many of these women grew up in households where they continually saw their mothers beaten or abused in other ways by their fathers, many came to expect little better for themselves. Numerous women who were sexually abused as young children tolerated extreme degrees of abuse in their marriages. They often sought aid only when their lives or the lives of their children became seriously jeopardized. Being raped as well as severely beaten by their husbands was not an uncommon occurrence.

In submitting to the demands of their husbands and lovers, however unreasonable, these women hoped to earn the care and protection of which they had been deprived in their childhoods. Unfortunately, because they selected men like their father-aggressors, they often found themselves in the frustrating position of asking for kindness and warmth from men who were incapable of giving it.

By continually adopting the role of the victim, these

women tend to place themselves in losing situations again and again. They repeatedly attempt to lose themselves in the love of a strong, overpowering male who they always hope will prove to be the "good father," but who more often than not turns out to be very much like their abuser.

The end result is often a feeling of hopelessness that leads to further self-destructive actions. Many such women have a history of abortive suicide attempts. Unwittingly, they seem to become caught up in a cycle of punishing themselves for a childhood crime they did not commit, but of which they were victims.

As children, incest victims also suffer a great deal of distress, many exhibit emotional disturbances. These children often experience guilt, shame, anxiety, and feelings of worthlessness. Some become hostile or demonstrate aggressive behavior and have difficulty in getting along well with others at school. Most of these children appear to be intensely afraid of being abandoned by their parents.

Parents who abuse their children sexually offer a variety of excuses to condone their actions. Some fathers have even gone as far as to suggest that their young daughters were in fact temptresses who actually seduced them. While it is true that children do have sexual feelings and do seek affection and attention from adults, it is the adult's responsibility to respond to the child's feelings and gestures in an appropriate manner. Exploiting the child for the parent's own sexual gratification is inappropriate, to say the least.

Studies of incestuous families indicate that there is often a high degree of marital or sexual discord between the parents. The fathers described their wives as cold or ungiving and claimed that their wives drove them to commit the incestuous act. However, studies reveal that fathers who were guilty of sexually abusing their offspring were generally able to demand sex from their wives as well.

Studies also frequently show that the mother may be ill, incapacitated, or in some way emotionally distant from her children and husband. In the family's effort to fill this void, many of the mother's traditional duties may fall to the eldest daughter. Thus the eldest daughter may take over a good deal of the housework and childcare. It also becomes her job to provide comfort and emotional support to her brothers and sisters as well as to her father. As the daughter evolves into the "miniature mother" of the family, her father may view his own sexual demands of her as almost an extension of her role.

Such an exchange of roles between mother and daughter is generally considered psychologically destructive to the young girl's normal development. She becomes burdened with excessive responsibilities at too early an age and is robbed of appropriate experiences with her peers which are crucial to her growth into adulthood.

In families in which incest occurs there is usually an extreme lack of maternal protectiveness on the mother's part. Strong, healthy, well-adjusted mothers refuse to be silent bystanders to the sexual exploitation of their children. Mothers in incestuous families are generally powerless within that structure to effect change. They often tolerate many forms of abuse themselves and feel unable to control their spouse's actions in any way.

The mothers of incest victims tend to be women with passive personalities who are oppressed by dominating, patriarchal husbands. These women are usually extremely dependent on and subservient to their husbands. Many of them suffer from psychological or emotional difficulties that make survival on their own appear to them as an unlikely possibility. Therefore, they attempt to preserve their place in the family at any cost.

If the price of maintaining the marriage includes closing their eyes to the sexual abuse of their own daughters, they may find it necessary to do so. Such women believe that they have no choice but to side with their husbands, regardless of their behavior. They believe that their first duty is to be loyal wives. The behavior of such mothers is generally dictated not by an absence of affection and compassion for their child, but rather by their own feelings of powerlessness and futility.

Many mothers of sexually abused daughters have been unable to fulfill their mothering function adequately. Some have been hospitalized for long periods due to disabling illnesses. Others live as invalids at home. Due to psychological disorders, others appear to be withdrawn, eccentric, or unavailable to their children. Many such mothers seem to be overburdened with the care of numerous small children, socially isolated, and economically dependent on their husbands. In general, the women seem ill-equipped to challenge their husband's domination in any area. In most incest cases studied, the lack of a strong, competent, responsible mother allowed the young girls to more readily become targets for an incestuous relationship initiated by their fathers.

The taboo against incest is universal. Every culture in human society forbids it. From a biological viewpoint, the purpose behind the incest taboo is the prevention of inbreeding. The prohibition of unrestricted sexual union among kin serves to regulate reproduction. According to the biological explanation, the disadvantages of inbreeding are numerous; a high incidence of congenital abnormalities, mental retardation, and stillbirths often result from such unions.

Anthropologically, the incest taboo is thought to help maintain and preserve the family structure. By governing all forms of sexual expression within the family unit, various disruptive sexual rivalries are minimized. If it is unthinkable for a boy to engage in sexual relations with his mother, rivalry with his brothers and father is minimized. Peace, order, and the family's hierarchal structure may be better maintained.

Families that have violated the incest taboo do not always appear to the outsider to be deviant. Many present a fairly solid front of respectability. Often the fathers have a stable employment history and the family may attend church services regularly and participate in related social functions. In most of the families studied in which incest had been committed, the traditional divisions of labor existed among family members. The men were most often regarded as the breadwinners, while the women were the homemakers. The father usually presided over the family unit as the unquestioned head of household. Roles were quite distinctly defined and were usually rigidly adhered to. Many former child-incest victims reported that they remembered that their fathers always discouraged their mothers from engaging in activities outside of the home or from forming new social contacts. The girls themselves were strongly discouraged from making new friends or from engaging in extracurricular activities at school.

It is not uncommon for incestuous fathers to dominate their families through the use of violence. Many men who sexually abuse their daughters are also guilty of beating their wives and children. At times, one child may be singled out for repeated unwarranted punishment, while siblings more favored by the father are spared.

One of the reasons incest may not be evident to outsiders is that the fathers often tend to restrict their violent behavior to the home. They try to hold themselves in check in their outside interactions, while they allow themselves to be out of control in the privacy of their own home. These men realize that their wives and children will not present strong opposition to their rule. As a result, they have an ideal setting in which to indulge their appetite for domination. However, when such men do become involved in confrontations with other men who are their equals, they tend to be submissive and will usually give in.

Alcoholism is extremely common among incestuous

fathers. It is difficult to determine the role drinking plays in the sexual abuse of these men's daughters. There are many alcoholic fathers who do not have incestuous relationships with their female children. However, through questioning, numerous alcoholic fathers who had sexually abused their daughters indicated that their drinking problem did not prompt them to engage in incest. Rather, they stated that they had planned their actions in advance and at times had used liquor to lower their reserve and invoke the courage to actually go through with the act.

Many fathers who sexually abuse their children seem to hold to the delusion that they have a right to initiate their daughters into sexual activities. Some will even assert that their actions were of an educational nature, telling the girls that they were preparing them for marriage or teaching them the facts of life. These fathers often call intercourse their special secret game. If the girls protest, their parent may try to manipulate them emotionally, claiming that the daughter is a spoiled child and selfish in her attitude. Incestuous fathers may tend to stress to their daughters that any good girl would want to make her daddy feel good.

Once incestuous relationships begin, they tend to be of long duration. The fathers will interact sexually with their daughters at every available opportunity. In spite of the daughters' reluctance, it is not uncommon for an incestuous bond to continue for three years or longer.

Many of the men who commit incestuous acts find sexually abusing their daughter to be more rewarding than having an extramarital affair with an adult woman. Having sex with his child tends to make the sexually abusive father feel strong and powerful. As the girls are often virgins with little or no experience, the father need not feel that his performance as a sexual partner is being judged and evaluated unfavorably in comparison to others.

In addition, the father's sexual satisfaction may be intensified as he indulges in a secret and forbidden act. In some cases, the child's unhappiness and feelings of oppression may actually serve to increase the father's sexual excitement. Incest, as well as numerous other sex crimes, is actually an exercise in power and domination. Feeling that he can master and rule another individual may prove to be even more gratifying to the aggressor than any sexual pleasure derived from intercourse.

In most cases, incest victims long for their mothers to rescue them, but those who do attempt to confide in their mothers are usually disappointed in the response. Even when they are confronted with the realities of what is happening to their daughters in their own home, these women are usually still unable to help their children. Some refuse to believe their daughters' claims; others who do believe the girls feel too frightened or dependent on their husbands to take action. The mothers themselves feel helpless and, as a result, allow their daughters to be sacrificed for their husband's desire and whim.

If the incestuous relationship is begun during or continues into the daughter's adolescence, the girls may begin to exhibit some signs of rebelliousness. The incestuous fathers may in turn become extremely jealous and fearful of competition for their daughters from boys outside the home.

Incestuous fathers attempt to prevent their daughters from forming normal social contacts with their peers. Some try to keep their daughters from having dates, going to parties, or wearing make-up or alluring clothing. Although they themselves seduced their own children, these fathers tend to view their daughters as promiscuous and untrustworthy. They wish to remain their child's sole sex object.

It is not uncommon for the incest victim to come to believe, after a time, that the only way to escape her intolerable situation is to find another powerful male figure. A great number of these girls become pregnant without benefit of marriage or tend to marry at an unusually early age. Often such girls see marriage as their ticket to freedom.

When a sexually abusive father does lose his victim to another man, it is not uncommon for him to compensate for the loss by sexually molesting another daughter.

Brothers within this type of family unit usually escape their father's sexual abuse. However, many such boys come to identify strongly with their aggressor-fathers. Research has borne out that often boys who grew up in sexually abusive home environments later molested their own children when they themselves became fathers.

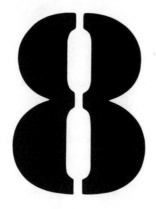

The Double Bind: Finding A Suitable Escape from an Intolerable Situation

We live in a society that is basically unsympathetic in its attitude to teenagers. As indicated earlier, the image of an abused child is that of someone who is slight, helpless, and innocent, who must remain at the mercy of his tormentor and has no alternatives available to him.

Abused teenagers do not evoke the same image and protective response. The mass media often reinforce this image of the "difficult-to-handle adolescent" with numerous stories of teenagers as troublemakers. As a group, adolescents are, on the whole, not completely trusted and their needs and desires are not always taken seriously.

If a teenager reports an instance of abuse, he may find that people tend to be suspicious rather than sympathetic. Some people continue to believe that due to a teenager's size and strength, it is not possible to really abuse him.

An abused adolescent may not present a very pretty or appealing picture. Due to low self-esteem, these individuals may have forsaken adequate grooming techniques and often may be dirty or unkempt. Many lack verbal and social skills. If they are frightened or confused by their plight, they may delay reporting incidents of abuse to outside authority figures. Then, as time passes, their stories may seem less accurate or believable.

Since such youths may have modeled their own behavior after that of their abusive parents, they may have adopted an abusive demeanor themselves, and may not be completely aware of how they come across to others. As a result, they may alienate the very people whose help they need by dealing with them in a harsh or ungrateful manner. The effects of abuse may inadvertently serve as a barrier to aid they so desperately need.

Maltreated youngsters may come to the attention of outside authorities not because of their own problems, but because of the violent or antisocial acts they have committed due to their abusive home lives. Randomly aggressive, violent acts do not elicit sympathy. Instead, they may actually provoke anger in those outside the home.

Another obstacle that often prevents the maltreated adolescent from getting the help he needs is the generally recognized, or at least presumed, unity and integrity of the individual family unit. "Father knows best" is more than the theme of an outdated television show; it is a fundamental concept in the American way of life. Intervention by outside forces is often regarded as an intrusion into the privacy of the family and a violation of the blood bond.

Maltreated teenagers may find themselves locked in an intricate double bind. Their families are supposed to help them resolve their problems, but when life within that very family unit presents insurmountable problems, the young person is faced with a serious dilemma. If he dares to ask for help from the outside, he may be viewed as disrespectful, disloyal, and destructive to his family.

There are not nearly enough services available to aid abused young people in their plight. Shelters for runaways, emergency crisis hotlines, and therapeutic group homes have proved to be helpful at times, but unfortunately such services are still far too few in number to offer any genuine assistance on a vast national level. In many states, conventional child welfare services involving a caretaker and/or foster placement operate under an extremely heavy caseload.

Some methods of intervention and help are thought to be more effective than others. Group homes for teenagers that are situated within a community have frequently been found to be advantageous to youthful residents. In most instances, these homes are staffed by social-work professionals who use their counseling skills to try to help the residents learn how to successfully live with and relate to others.

There is a tremendous difference between living in a home of this type and placement within a conventional institutional setting. In a small group home, residents share a setting that is similar to family life. They often develop close bonds with their counselors as well as with the other residents. Living in an actual community affords them an opportunity to develop the skills needed for adult life.

There are not enough group homes to serve everyone who might benefit from living in one. Some of the available group homes are privately owned and are quite costly. An expense of this kind is out of the financial reach of many families who are in need of such a service.

The two other most common alternatives for adolescents who must be removed from an intolerable home setting are foster care or placement in an institution.

Many adolescents who have had to leave their homes

because of abuse have been placed in foster-care settings by social welfare agencies. Placements for teenagers are difficult to obtain, as many foster parents think the teen years are troublesome. They prefer taking in younger children. Still another problem may arise for the young person placed in a foster home, in that if he is not happy with the situation he may have the resourcefulness to run away or to behave in such an unruly manner that his foster parents feel compelled to give him up.

Many states do not review foster placement situations as often as might be desirable. If an adolescent feels that he has been placed in an inappropriate foster setting, it may be difficult for him to express his complaint in a way that will ensure a swift, direct remedy.

The teenager is not usually an active participant in the choice of foster placement. To make matters worse, even if a suitable relative outside of the adolescent's immediate family is willing to care for the youth, there is usually no financial aid available. As a result, in less affluent areas, fewer teenagers are taken in by relatives than might be hoped.

Another alternative for stable, mature teenagers, who are able to care for themselves financially and emotionally, is living independently outside the home. A minor can legally live away from home if he becomes emancipated. Once emancipated, the parents' rights as the young person's guardians are terminated, and the youth is then given the same legal status as any adult in our society. He is now fully responsible for himself and his actions.

Emancipation is not always easily attained. The young

person is required to be completely able to provide for himself and must have the approval of his parents or legal guardians. In many instances, the parents are reluctant to relinquish control over their offspring and successfully block this arrangement.

A young person who has been maltreated at home, but feels he is unable to come up with a viable alternative living arrangement, may find that his oppressive home life is more than he is able to handle. When every other path seems blocked, he may decide to run away.

No one knows exactly how many runaways are attempting to survive alone out in the world, but recent estimates have been as high as over 100,000 per annum. Runaways differ greatly in their commitment to leaving home permanently. While most runaways are gone for only a few days and tend to remain within a few miles of their own homes, some do make a real break with their families and immediate neighborhoods. These teenagers get more than just a fleeting glimpse of life on the street.

Runaways tend to fall into three general categories. The first category might be best described as those who have left their homes in search of glamour and adventure. The second grouping includes those who cannot remain at home because of their own severe emotional problems. The last category consists of runaways who run to escape from abuse.

The first type of runaway may be somewhat of a thrill seeker, in search of newness and excitement. Although relationships between family members within his home unit may not reach ideal standards, he is not a victim of abuse. Problems within his family may be related to poor interpersonal communication and may be improved or resolved through family therapy. This type of runaway is the most likely of the three categories to return home. Often, he initially has the best inner resources to draw upon and may find himself least scathed by the experience of running away.

The second type of runaway suffers from severe emotional problems, which may or may not be connected to abuse. This type of person may experience very severe depression or anxiety or he may find himself prone to mood swings. He will have experienced difficulty in relating to others and may not always be in close touch with reality. His escape from home may be an unconscious attempt to escape from his own tumultuous feelings. Unfortunately, however, his troubled thoughts travel with him. The forecast for his future is perhaps less optimistic than for the two other types of runaways.

The last group of young people have fled their homes to escape abuse. The maltreatment may be emotional, physical, or sexual, but the result is the same. Here a young person has attempted to leave an unbearably painful situation. Some researchers have estimated that over a third of all runaways are victims of abuse. To these young people, life alone on the street is more desirable than remaining at home.

Some maltreatment victims who are forced to live out on the street have actually been expelled from their home by their parents. Many times the young person is driven out after enduring years of abuse. The abusive or neglectful parent may move to a smaller residence or change his romantic partner and suddenly decide that his offspring has become a burden that he wishes to shed. Such a parent will often start an argument or degrade the young person unjustly as an excuse for throwing the child out. The blame and recrimination he foists on the child are actually just a defense to justify his own inappropriate behavior.

If there should be an unexpected change in the parent's life, he may try to bring the child back into the home. If the parent's spouse or companion abandons him or if he loses his job, he may feel wounded at a vulnerable time and may hope to lean emotionally on his child once again. In effect, he recreates the same destructive mode of behavior that originally led to the abusive situation. Upon his return, the child may find himself no better off than he was on the street.

A runaway adolescent may often find himself at the mercy of forces beyond his control. Each year there are hundreds of reported cases of runaway teens who have been raped, robbed, maimed, molested, beaten, even murdered. Police have conservatively estimated that thousands of these incidents go unreported every year.

Without funds or their own means of transportation, many teens on the run have resorted to hitchhiking—a practice that has cost innumerable runaways their lives. Being under age and having few marketable skills, these young people often have extreme difficulty finding legitimate employment.

It is common for runaways to venture into crime. They begin to shoplift and even become initiated into various con games. Many become involved in drug deal-

ing, passing bad checks, burglary, pornography, and prostitution.

Not every abused youth becomes a runaway, or remains in his home situation, or becomes emancipated, or
is placed in foster care. There is another alternative, but
not one that portends a very bright future for victims of
maltreatment. Many abuse victims end up spending a
portion of their lives in institutions. Whether they act out
in violence against an abusive home situation or are introduced to crime as runaways, the end result may be a
stint in an institution of some sort.

Teenagers in institutions may at times be the object
of mistreatment and abuse by both other inmates and
staff members. Although more recently some reforms
have been introduced, often the food and sanitary conditions in many of these places have been substandard.
Medical care is often inadequate. Some young inmates
have been beaten or raped or have undergone severe
punishment. Some have suffered all sorts of humiliations
and indignities. Inmates may, at best, be cursed, belittled,
or threatened for little cause.

More than one million children and adolescents re-
side in institutions of various kinds, including detention
centers, temporary and permanent shelters, and centers
for the retarded and disabled. Many states do not even
make counseling services available to youths before the
decision is made to have them institutionalized. If their
placement in an institution is the outcome of an abusive
home life, few social services are available to improve the
family situation before the youngster's return.

What Can
Be Done?

In recent years numerous approaches have been suggested to help curb the problem of abusive families in America. Perhaps the most obvious answer is to remove the youngster from the destructive home environment. Although this may certainly be the most expedient remedy for the dangers of a highly volatile situation, it may not be the best overall solution for the majority of youths who are victims of maltreatment.

As was discussed in the last chapter, available placement situations outside the home are not plentiful. In addition, there is often a great deal of bureaucracy and time-consuming paperwork to go through, and many states do not have the staff or time to ensure that such placements will offer the child an environment that is genuinely superior to the home situation.

It is commonly thought that whenever possible, abuse victims should be kept within the mainstream of society. Since most American children grow up within their own nuclear families, maltreated children might feel more like "everyone else" if they could stay in a family setting. As a result, numerous agencies and organizations have sprung up to assist abusive families as a unit.

One such group is Parents Anonymous, founded in Los Angeles, California, in 1970. It is a self-help support group, similar in orientation and design to Alcoholics Anonymous. The basis of the organization is the premise that people facing similar dilemmas can pool their resources and work together to help themselves, their children, and other group members. At PA, parents have an opportunity to share their feelings with others who have had similar experiences. Within their group, the members need not fear the judgment and condemnation of people who may not fully understand all of the circumstances that led to the abusive behavior.

PA provides an opportunity for member parents to let off steam as stress accumulates. The members may exchange phone numbers, and if a parent should feel that the inner turmoil he is experiencing may explode into violence against a child, he can call another member to "talk out" his feelings. Experienced PA members help the new parents become acclimated to the program, who then become responsible for newcomers.

PA teaches abusive parents that it's all right to ask for help. Parents are encouraged to learn how to deal with their negative feelings as well as how to redirect destructive tendencies into constructive channels.

There are no waiting lists or red tape in Parents Anonymous. A crisis need not erupt for a parent in trouble to receive the aid and support of the other group members. New members are welcomed into the group at any time. There are currently more than 1,000 chapters of Parents Anonymous across the country. In addition, PA has a toll-free, 24-hour hot line for parents in crisis who feel they may lash out at their children. In California call (800) 352-0386. Elsewhere call (800) 421-0353. Besides sponsoring parents' groups, programs for abused young people are also available.

Another organization dedicated to improving the quality of life for young people is the Children's Defense Fund. The Children's Defense Fund is a nationwide nonprofit organization working to change the conditions that force children to go to bed hungry, destitute, or without care. CDF pays particular attention to the needs of poor, minority, and disabled children.

Their staff includes researchers, lawyers, public-policy experts, and public advocates. These professionals specialize in the areas of child health, mental health, education, child welfare, foster care, income support, and jobs for youths and parents.

According to a Children's Defense Fund policy paper, the organization has concentrated its efforts in the following areas:

> In EDUCATION, CDF strives to get and keep children in school.
>
> In CHILD HEALTH, CDF tries to ensure that children have regular medical and dental care before they get sick.
>
> In CHILD WELFARE, CDF works to give the 500,000 children without homes a chance for permanent families and to keep families and children together.
>
> In CHILD CARE, CDF acts to expand the quality and quantity of child care options for parents, especially those who must work outside the home.
>
> In INCOME SUPPORT and JOBS, CDF tries to ensure that all families have the means to support themselves, and that all children have a chance to become productive, self-sufficient citizens in an increasingly technological society.

CDF reaches out to an active network of Americans who care about children and their future by

- *developing books and pamphlets on the needs of children and families*
- *providing information, research, seminars, and training assistance to state and local groups*
- *protecting children's rights in courts*
- *working to make sure children's programs receive their fair share of the federal budget*
- *monitoring federal and state policies to ensure that children receive the maximum benefits from federal programs*
- *publishing a monthly newsletter,* **CDF REPORTS,** *to keep people informed about children's needs and the changing federal scene*
- *building a children's constituency of parents, grandparents, teachers, professionals, advocates, and members of the religious community who can raise a voice for children's needs.*

Although CDF's main office is in Washington, D.C., it reaches out to towns and cities across the country to find out and influence what is happening to children. CDF helps others who work with children, monitors the effects of changes in national and state policies, and helps to organize those working to influence what happens to children in their community, their state, and their nation. The Children's Defense Fund maintains state offices in Mississippi and Ohio and has developed cooperative projects with groups in many states, and works closely with a range of national and state networks.

Another organization created to help youths in trouble is the National Network of Runaway and Youth

Services, Inc. The National Network of Runaway and Youth Services grew out of the urgent concerns of people across the nation who were aware of the large number of adolescents in danger on the streets. In some communities, concerned citizens, clergymen, and parents were joined by social-work professionals to develop programs designed to meet the needs of these youths and their families. Those people and programs began to locate each other in the early '70s, and by 1974 had begun to organize as state and national networks. In 1977 a small amount of money was secured for national staff. The membership grew, and the Network began to make an impact on public policy as well as to share information about program design among its members.

Most programs like these started in local churches, YMCAs and YWCAs or other community centers. They were not part of government structures, but developed because people saw children in need of help, and they responded to those needs. Such responses were later given the name "alternative programs," because they were correctly perceived as alternatives to the traditional government agencies such as Child Welfare, criminal justice, and mental health systems.

After the discovery of the bodies of youths murdered by a sadistic killer in Houston as well as other atrocities committed elsewhere, the public was aroused enough to realize that there were many children missing from their homes and that very few communities had any way of helping their families. Congress responded to this concern by passing the Runaway Youth Act of 1974. This legislation has funded up to 169 private, nonprofit programs that currently shelter 45,000 young people annually—less than 5 percent of the estimated number of young people in crisis.

The National Network also grew, adding new runaway programs and other youth and family service programs to its membership; in 1982 there were 96 individual agency members and 15 coalitions, with a combined membership of well over 600 programs.

The National Network has a regular newsletter and other membership communication systems. It holds an annual meeting where members elect officers and select policy and program issues for the coming year. It is a member of the National Collaboration for Youth, along with such organizations as Scouts, Camp Fire, and YMCA and YWCA. Network goals are to bring national attention to the needs of youngsters in crisis and to assist communities developing economical programs of high quality to meet those needs. Funding comes from membership dues, foundations and corporations, and private contributions from individuals who share the group's concerns.

The National Network is the only organization that has its primary focus on the issue of the plight of youth on the street. It strives to increase public awareness and understanding of this problem and to provide leadership to communities who want to help care for their children.

The organization has published the following fact sheet about its efforts.

I. THE NATIONAL NETWORK IS A MEMBERSHIP ORGANIZATION OF 600 PRIVATE COMMUNITY

*AGENCIES SERVING RUNAWAY, HOMELESS,
AND OTHERWISE TROUBLED YOUTH IN 45
STATES.*

- *Programs are open 24 hours a day, 7 days a week.*
- *The organizations cooperate with police, courts, and local
  Child Protective groups. Many programs are sponsored by
  local YMCA or YWCA's, churches, or other traditional
  groups seeking to provide relevant services to troubled youth
  of their community.*

The services provided include:

*1. Food, shelter, and safety in a homelike setting or in private
(often volunteer) foster homes for a period of up to 30 days.*

*2. Immediate crisis intervention counseling by phone or in
person for youth and families 24 hours a day, 7 days a week.*

*3. Short term individual, group, and family counseling to
persons or families in need regardless of stated problem or income
level. Goals are clarified, options are assessed, and plans are made
to deal with problems confronting the youth or family.*

*4. Case work to assist young people and their families in
understanding their problems and carrying out a course of action.*

*5. Referral and advocacy services to assist youth and their
families in meeting their goals. Referrals are most often made for
specialized legal, medical, psychiatric, and educational assistance
when needed.*

*6. Aftercare and follow-through to assure that plans set in
motion are working; to redefine goals if necessary; and to support
the youth and families in their efforts to help themselves.*

Depending on local need, many programs have developed additional services such as streetwork, independent living for homeless teens, group homes, long-term

family therapy, parent training and support networks, employment services, teen pregnancy and parenting services, and youth-run businesses.

The goals of the organization's services are to
1. Reunite youth with their families and strengthen family relationships.
2. Assist youth in understanding their problems and deciding on responsible courses of action.
3. Prevent unnecessary institutionalization of young people and prevent family breakdown through early intervention.
4. Promote improved and expanded community support for troubled adolescents and their families where necessary.

The Network programs serve approximately one-half million young people annually. Three hundred thousand of these youths receive shelter, and the balance are reached through preventive or walk-in services. They come from all walks of life and present a complex range of problems. According to the organization's data:

- *Of the youth sheltered 45% are runaways; 30% were ejected from their homes or left home by mutual consent, 5% were considering running away, and the remaining 20% were already placed outside of their parents' home through court, welfare or psychiatric involvement.*
- *Over 30% of the youth sheltered report child abuse or incest episodes; 55% report family communication problems and 25% report family disruption not involving the youth (i.e. parental alcoholism, marital disputes, etc.).*
- *71.4% are white, 21.1% are Black, and 6.4% are Hispanic.*

- *36% have run across state or local jurisdictional lines.*
- *40% are school drop-outs, truant, suspended or expelled. The majority report some difficulty in school.*
- *65% are female and the average age is 15 years.*

The organization states that "the youth touched by our service are the tip of the iceberg of the extensive problems faced by youth in America. Many of the problems are interrelated and are experienced by the same small but significant group of adolescents. Each frightening figure is symptomatic of a cry for help and a statement that for some young people growing up in America is not working."

- *1½ million American teenagers run away each year or are in a crisis in which they need care outside of their home.*
- *Adolescents are the only American age group for which the death rate is increasing. The three leading causes of death are violent accidents, homicide, and suicide, respectively. Suicide rates have increased by 75% since 1968 as compared to 17% for all age groups.*
- *300,000 young people were involved in the pornographic industry in a 1.5 year period. In Minnesota, data shows that 46% of the juveniles involved in prostitution were runaways, and in the District of Columbia the rate was seven out of ten.*

The National Network of Runaway and Youth Services, Inc., is organized into ten regional networks of member programs. The following is a listing of the available programs and where they may be contacted.

92

Region I: Vermont, Connecticut, Maine, New Hampshire, Rhode Island, Massachusetts
Youth In Crisis, 3030 Park Avenue, Bridgeport, CT 06604
John Cottrell . . . .[203] 374-9471

Region II: New York, New Jersey, Puerto Rico, Virgin Islands
Runaway And Homeless Youth Advocacy Project, 444 W. 56th Street, New York, NY 10019
Stu Aaronson . . . .[212] 489-3588

Region III: Delaware, District of Columbia, Maryland, Virginia, West Virginia, Pennsylvania
Voyage House, 311 S. Juniper St., Suite 1000-10th Fl., Philadelphia, PA 19107
Roberta Hacker . . . .[215] 545-0166

Region IV: Alabama, Florida, Georgia, Kentucky, Mississippi, North Carolina, South Carolina, Tennessee
The Family Link, P.O. Box 40437, Memphis, TN 38104
Bill Myers . . . .[901] 725-6911

Region V: Illinois, Indiana, Minnesota, Ohio, Wisconsin, Michigan
Walker's Point Youth & Family Center, 732 S. 21st St., Milwaukee, WI 53215
Richard Ward . . . .[414] 647-8200

Region VI: Louisiana, New Mexico, Oklahoma, Texas, Arkansas
Youth Services for Oklahoma County, 1219 Classen, Oklahoma City, OK 73106
Sharon Wiggins . . . .[405] 235-7537

Region VII: Iowa, Kansas, Missouri, Nebraska
Youth In Need, 529 Jefferson St., St. Charles, MO
63301
Sue Schneider ....[314] 724-7171

Region VIII: Colorado, Montana, North Dakota, South
Dakota, Utah, Wyoming
Mt. Plains Youth Services Coalition, P.O. Box 1242,
Pierre, SD 57501
Doug Herzog ....[605] 224-8696

Region IX: Arizona, California, Hawaii, Nevada, Guam,
Territorial Trusts
San Diego Youth & Community Servs., 1214 28th St.,
San Diego, CA 92102
Liz Goldsmith ....[619] 232-5156

Region X: Alaska, Idaho, Oregon, Washington
The Shelter, 1545 12th Ave., S., Seattle, WA 98144
Linda Reppond ....[206] 328-0902

At-Large: Racial Minority Caucus
Project Contact, 315 East 10th St., New York, NY
10009
Madelyn McDonald ....[212] 533-3570

At-Large: Sexual Minorities
N.Y.C. Runaway Hotline, 2 Lafeyette St., New York,
NY 10001
Marsha Day ....[212] 577-7700

National Chairperson
Detroit Transit Alternatives, 2211 Woodward, Suite
1208, Detroit, MI 48204
Roy Jones ....[313] 869-4040

Chief Executive Officer
National Network of Runaway and Youth Services, Inc.,
905 6th St., SW, Suite 612, Washington, DC 20024
June Bucy ....[202] 488-0739

Activities of the national office of the Network include the following:
   1. *Educating policymakers on the needs of runaways, homeless
and alienated youth and the work of member centers.*
   2. *Informing member agencies of public policy trends, emerg-
ing service models and research results.*
   3. *Public education and resource development for member services.*
   4. *Maintaining a high quality of services and management
among member centers.*
   5. *Special training and research and demonstration projects.*

Activities of the Regional Networks include:

   1. *Training and mutual assistance among centers.*
   2. *Exchanging program, management, and legislative models.*
   3. *Providing mutual support among small community agencies.*
   4. *Facilitating interstate and inter-region referrals of youth
who run across state lines.*

The Kempe National Center for the Prevention and

Treatment of Child Abuse and Neglect at 1205 Oneida Street, Denver, Colorado 80220, (303) 321-3963, is yet another organization formed to assist mistreated youths. The Kempe Center was established in 1972 to provide extensive and up-to-date education, research, and clinical services in the field of child abuse and neglect. The center's staff includes multidisciplinary professionals and lay people. The center grew out of the Child Protection Team, originated in 1958 at the University of Colorado Medical Center, under the direction of C. Henry Kempe, M.D., pediatrician, with Brandt F. Steele, M.D., psychiatrist. They originally became concerned about children who were hospitalized for nonaccidental injuries. Dr. Kempe presented his findings to the American Medical Association and the battered child syndrome became a recognized diagnosis.

The program's current services include:

- *Child Protection Team at University Hospital, University of Colorado Health Sciences Center.*
- *Therapeutic Playschool for Children ages 2 to 5.*
- *Family Evaluation Program —Comprehensive assessment of families, providing treatment recommendations, consultations with other professionals and agencies, court reports and testimony as needed. Includes all types of disturbed family relationships, failure to thrive, sexual abuse, physical and emotional abuse or neglect, parent-child interaction, and mother-child attachment difficulties.*
- *Ongoing therapy for children and adults; individual, marital, and group treatment.*

- *Phone consultation regarding cases with pediatric, psychiatric, psychological, legal, social work, or early childhood expertise as needed.*
- *Resource services. Audiovisual rental, circulating library, publication sales, and topic searches.*
- *On-site consultation regarding program development.*
- *Training for professional and lay workers.*
- *Springtime Foundation which provides support for adults who were mistreated as children.*

The American Humane Association (AHA), another organization concerned with improving life for children, has issued the following statement about itself and its goals.

The American Humane Society with national headquarters in Denver, Colorado, is a private, nonprofit organization founded in 1877. For over 100 years, AHA has been concerned with the protection of children and the prevention of child maltreatment. Its approach to the problem has evolved over the years and represents adaptations to changes in society.

Early efforts were of a broad social action nature and were concerned with the promotion of child labor laws, creation of shelter care for children who were separated from their homes, detention facilities to keep children out of jails, abolishment of baby farms, support of special courts for children, and promotion of child protective services to alleviate child neglect and abuse. The early child protection system rested on investigation and child rescue through placement of "cruelly treated" children in foster boarding and institutions.

Since that time, Child Protective Services has developed into a specialized area of Child Welfare. As perceived by

AHA, *it should be concerned with identifying, treating, and preventing neglect, abuse, and exploitation of children by "reaching out" with social services to stabilize family life. It should seek to preserve the family unit by strengthening parental capacity for adequate child care.*

AHA's Children's Division has consistently focused on the protection of children and the strengthening through support and development of direct service providers. The agencies we work with are largely the child protective service agencies mandated to identify and protect abused and neglected children.

We believe the effective delivery of child protective services depends on the integration of a host of rather diverse factors, ranging from the skill of the individual child protective services worker to the establishment of a political climate wherein the welfare of children and their families is recognized as a national priority.

In accordance with this reality, American Humane undertakes a unique yet well-rounded approach to improving the child protective services system through a variety of research programs, evaluation, training, consultation, public education, and advocacy activities.

The AHA works closely with public social service agencies to develop programs, train their workers and supervisors, promote standards for enhancing the quality of practice, evaluate services, advocate for children and families, undertake research, and provide technical assistance to states and localities in the management and use of information.

Our research and evaluation program is focused on analyzing the system's capability with respect to effective performance. This entails expanding the base of knowledge about child abuse per se as well as increasing the understanding of how the system operates on local, state, and national levels.

Our training and consultation program is directed toward enhancing the overall capability of the child protection system by providing those responsible for the delivery of service with the tools required for effectively helping families. This involves us with state and provincial officials and child welfare program administrators as well as supervisors and on-the-line workers. Over time we will be designing curricula for other disciplines, such as law enforcement, schools, mental health, and nursing.

Finally we recognize that it is the general public through their elected officials who make the decisions with regard to financial and political support of the child protective services system. Therefore we try to maintain an active program of public education and advocacy through our publications, response to information requests, use of the media, participation in professional conferences, and speaking before community groups. We also rely on our Washington, D.C. office to keep our organization and our membership better informed of pending legislation and advocacy needs related to children's issues.

To sum up, our programs involve EDUCATION, AD-VOCACY, CONSULTATION, RESEARCH, AND PUB-LICATIONS.

- *We can provide the most authoritative statistics on the nature and extent of reported child abuse and neglect.*
- *We can provide comprehensive specialized training of workers and supervisors. Last year alone we trained more than 1,400 people in a variety of American states and two Canadian provinces.*
- *We can provide a professional response when called on by state and local agencies for expert consultation, program evaluation, and technical assistance.*
- *We provide expert testimony and participate in the submis-*

*sion of legal briefs to enhance understanding and judgment
in child protection cases when called upon by the courts.*

- *We provide local and national specialized training institutes around issues such as sexual abuse and incest, the management of cases, accountability, malpractice, and legal, and medical issues, to name a few.*

- *We encourage professional development through our annual conference which draws hundreds of child welfare professionals throughout the United States and Canada each year.*

- *We are committed to an ongoing effort to provide information to the public on the critical, current issues and topics related to child welfare.*

The American Humane Society may be contacted at 9725 East Hampden, Denver, Colorado 80231 (303) 695-0811.

The National Center on Child Abuse and Neglect/ Children's Bureau was established by the Child Abuse Prevention and Treatment Act of 1974. The long-range goal of NCCAN/CB, which is implicit in the act, is to reduce the incidence of child abuse and neglect in the United States. To accomplish this goal, the agency has legislative authority to pursue three basic objectives, which they have defined as follows:

1. Increased knowledge and understanding of child abuse and neglect problems and solutions, through
   a. the development of more precise definitions of child abuse and neglect;
   b. the determination of the extent and severity of child abuse and neglect; and

c. the examination of the causes and effects of child abuse and neglect.

2. An integrated service delivery system which uses all of the relevant human services to meet the needs of children and families endangered by child abuse and neglect, through

a. the mobilization and coordination of effective services to prevent child abuse and neglect;

b. the effective identification and reporting of known or suspected cases of child abuse and neglect; and

c. the provision of timely, humane, and effective child protective intervention.

3. High quality services for families to prevent and treat child abuse and neglect, through

a. improvement of the quality of services provided by child protective services workers;

b. improvement of the quality of services provided by other human service, law enforcement and judicial personnel; and

c. community support for agencies and organizations which provide services to prevent and treat child abuse and neglect.

NCCAN/CB implements steps to accomplish the above objectives in the following ways:

1. By providing leadership to agencies and professionals working in the field;

2. By acting as a catalyst to stimulate program improvements;

3. By educating professionals, paraprofessionals, and the general public about the prevention and treatment of child abuse and neglect; and

4. By coordinating federal and state prevention and treatment efforts.

101

The National Center On Child Abuse and Neglect/ Children's Bureau can be contacted by writing to the Office of Human Development Services, Department of Health and Human Services, P.O. Box 1182, Washington, D.C., 20013.

The Clearinghouse on Child Abuse and Neglect Information was established by the National Center on Child Abuse and Neglect to collect, process, and, most importantly, to spread information on child abuse and neglect. The Clearinghouse serves a wide range of clients, including other governmental agencies, Congress, state and local agencies, involved professionals, and concerned members of the public.

At the core of the Clearinghouse is a computerized data base that contains several types of information related to child abuse and neglect. They are as follows:

- *Published Documents—Bibliographic data and abstracts of journal articles, books, dissertations, reports, and other publications about the medical, legal, mental health, social welfare, and educational aspects of child abuse and neglect.*
- *Court Case Decisions—Summaries of important court decisions in child abuse and neglect cases.*
- *Research Projects—Descriptions of ongoing projects in child abuse and neglect funded by federal, state, and local government agencies and by private organizations.*
- *Programs—Descriptions of programs that provide services to abused or neglected children and their parents or families.*
- *Audiovisual Materials—Descriptions of films, filmstrips, videotapes, audiocassettes, and other items dealing with child abuse and neglect.*

- *State Laws—Excerpts from current state and territorial child abuse and neglect laws, including reporting laws and the welfare, criminal, and juvenile court codes.*
- *State Child Protective Service Systems—A collection of narrative descriptions of each state's child protective service system.*

The Clearinghouse collection includes information in the following major subject areas in child abuse and neglect:

Definitions
Incidence and Prevalence
Psychology
Social Ecology
Prevention
Treatment
Effects
Programs and Agencies
Training and Public Awareness
Identification and Prediction
Reporting
Legal Rights, Responsibilities, and Procedures
Sexual Abuse

The Clearinghouse provides a number of services and products. These include bibliographies, custom searches, annual reviews, in-depth analyses, compilations of resource materials, and directories. For a current catalog of publications available from the Clearinghouse, write to:

NCCAN Children's Bureau, Department of Health and

Human Services, P.O. Box 1182, Washington, D.C., 20013.

The Child Abuse and Neglect Searching Service of the Clearinghouse replies to telephone and written inquiries for information. Inquiries may be telephoned to the Clearinghouse by using a special searchline number: (703) 558-8222.

Still another organization dedicated to easing the predicament of maltreated youth is the National Committee for the Prevention of Child Abuse. According to its description of its services:

> *The National Committee for the Prevention of Child Abuse (NCPCA) was established in 1972 in response to the increasing incidents of infant deaths due to purposely inflicted injury. At that time research showed that most child abuse programs focused on rehabilitation: the injured child was brought to the attention of medical, legal, and social service agencies after the abuse had occurred, often too late for help. NCPCA was formed to help* prevent *child abuse.*
>
> *NCPCA is concerned about the rights of all children to live and to mature normally—both physically and mentally—to do so with dignity, and to develop their individual potentials.*
>
> *NCPCA's programs are designed to expand knowledge about the prevention of child abuse and put that knowledge into action through the development of child abuse prevention programs in communities throughout the country. NCPCA's programs include public awareness, public education, a national network of concerned citizens, a variety of prevention programs, research and evaluation, and advocacy efforts.*

PUBLIC AWARENESS

To make the nation aware of the problem of child abuse, NCPCA, in conjunction with the Advertising Council, Inc., and the Campbell-Ewald Company, has developed public-service announcements for television, radio, newspapers, consumer magazines, business and trade journals, and transit and outdoor advertising display. Since 1976 the purposes have remained the same: to increase public awareness of the problem of child abuse and to tell how the problem can be prevented.

Although NCPCA is the sponsor, public-service announcements are designed for local use by bona fide groups at no cost.

Six continuous campaigns have been launched. The total estimated value of donated print space and radio and television air time is $160 million dollars.

PUBLIC EDUCATION

To educate the public about abuse, NCPCA publishes and distributes educational materials that deal with a variety of topics including child abuse, child abuse prevention, and parenting. Written by professionals from many fields, these materials are clear, precise, and conversational in their treatment of the subject matter. Some publications are available in both English and Spanish. The NCPCA Catalog, which describes the materials and gives ordering information, is available free upon request from the NCPCA Publishing Department, 332 South Michigan Avenue, Suite 1250, Chicago, Illinois. Public education is also facilitated through conferences and workshops, which serve as forums to exchange knowledge and experience, to develop cooperative efforts between agencies and individuals, to provide training for professionals and volunteers, and to determine future strategies that will improve prevention programs.

NATIONAL NETWORK OF CONCERNED CITIZENS

Child abuse is a community problem and can be prevented only at a community level. NCPCA works in communities through its chapters composed of volunteers in states across the country. Organized on a statewide or regional basis, each chapter includes representatives from civic groups, the business community, existing prevention and treatment programs, and other concerned individuals. This fusion of volunteers forms a network linking isolated programs and permitting the individuals to communicate, cooperate, and coordinate their resources to begin prevention programs where none exist or to improve existing programs. There are NCPCA chapters in the following locations: Alabama, Alaska, California, Colorado, Connecticut, District of Columbia, Georgia, Hawaii, Indiana, Iowa, Kansas, Kentucky, Michigan, Minnesota, Missouri, Nevada, New

Hampshire, New Jersey, New York, North Carolina, Oregon, Rhode Island, South Dakota, Tennessee, Texas, Virginia, Washington, and Wisconsin. NCPCA's national office offers technical assistance and consultative services to its chapters as well as to diverse agencies, programs, and individuals around the country.

This includes help in establishing prevention programs, and drafting and implementing legislative programs as well as in giving assistance in community organization, public awareness programs, raising funds, staff and board training, program development, and program evaluation. For further information on these chapters write or call NCPCA Chapter Development, 332 South Michigan Avenue, Suite 1250, Chicago, Illinois, (312) 663-3520.

PREVENTION PROGRAMS

The core of NCPCA activities is the development and implementation of community-based child abuse prevention programs. NCPCA is dedicated to programs that have an impact on the family before any child is abused, that can be easily duplicated in communities throughout the country, and that are cost-effective. NCPCA works closely with its chapters in the development of community-based programs such as:

Support Groups for New Parents—to aid in the early development of strong attachments between the new parent and the infant, and to promote family-centered birthing opportunities.

Education for Parents—to provide parents with information about child development and skills in child care as well as information about local social service and health resources.

Early and Regular Child and Family Screening and Treatment—to identify and deal with physical and developmental problems in children at an early age.

Child-Care Opportunities—such as day care centers—to provide respite for parents and socialization opportunities for children.

Programs for Abused Children and Young Adults—to minimize the longer-term effects on children and young adults who have been abused, and to reduce the likelihood of their becoming abusive parents.

Life Skills Training for Children and Young Adults—to equip young people with skills, knowledge, and experience necessary to cope with crises, to seek helping services, and to succeed in adulthood, particularly in the role of parent.

Neighborhood Support and Self-Help Groups—to reduce the social isolation so often associated with abuse,

NORTH HIGH
SCHOOL LIBRARY

particularly for higher-risk groups such as teenage parents.

Family Support Services, including crisis care such as hot-line counseling and related emergency services, as well as longer-term support such as alcohol and drug counseling—to provide families with what they need to cope with the stresses of life to stay together, particularly for parents of children of any age with special needs, such as the disabled child.

Community Organization Activities—to increase the availability of social service and health and education resources, as well as other supports that reduce family stress.

Public Information and Education on Child Abuse Prevention—to heighten the public's awareness of different types of abuse and to provide specific information on how the problem can be prevented.

For further information about the organization you may write directly to NCPCA, 332 S. Michigan Avenue, Suite 1250, Chicago, Illinois (312) 663-3520.

Reports of child abuse and neglect to the authorities may come from neighbors, relatives, friends, various professionals who come in contact with the child, or even the young victim himself. Offenses involving child abuse and neglect come under the jurisdiction of state law. Although every state has its own law against the abuse of children, the precise legal definitions of what actually constitutes abuse may vary from state to state.

The state laws all authorize at least one agency to answer and investigate reported cases of child abuse on a statewide basis. Often that agency is called the Department of Social Services or Child and Family Services. In many places, the reporting number for the state will be listed in the front pages of the telephone directory.

The purpose of the reporting process is to identify the young person in danger and to ensure his immediate safety. The agency should fully investigate the situation to determine if abuse or neglect is actually occurring, and then proceed with the appropriate measures to warrant that such actions against the child cease. If the child's life or safety is in immediate jeopardy, the child may be removed from the home by a court order. Regardless of whether or not the child is taken from the home, the investigating agency will propose a treatment program designed to strengthen the family unit and to help ensure that no further abuse occurs in the future.

A person who reports a case of suspected child abuse "in good faith" is guaranteed immunity from civil or criminal liability. In good faith means that the information is reported because the individual genuinely believes that a child either is or had been in jeopardy of being abused.

The current trend in treating abuse cases generally leans toward attempting to aid and strengthen the family unit as a whole. The abusive parent needs to learn new and constructive ways of relating to his child, and often

the abused child needs assistance in overcoming the emotional pain he may have been forced to deal with.

Putting the abusive parent behind bars may satisfy a need for revenge but does little to solve the problem on a long-term basis. Imprisonment will not teach an abusive parent how to better handle stress or work through his personal problems or tumultuous feelings. In addition, if a child is withdrawn from an abusive home, the family's fundamental problems may continue to go unaddressed. A well-integrated framework of support systems that includes self-help groups, social service agencies, friends and relatives, and parenting education programs is necessary if domestic violence is to be curbed.

In addition, changes on a community level must be implemented as well. Communities must provide adequate funding for their child protective services and must tailor existing agency programs to meet the needs of abused children and adolescents. For example, expanded crisis hot-line services across the country are needed, and there is still a scarcity of short-term shelters available to youths who need a quick and safe place to run to when a crisis erupts at home.

Communities can also aid the plight of abused young people by supporting and electing to office officials who support nonviolent child-rearing and are prepared to endorse legislation that reflects this philosophy.

Within recent years, more attention than ever before has been focused on the issue of child abuse and neglect. Numerous books as well as newspaper and magazine articles have been published on the subject. Every state in

the Union has strengthened its child abuse laws within the last ten years, and child-advocacy groups have sprung up across the nation.

However, the elimination of this widespread problem has only begun. No one can afford to sit back and believe that everything is already taken care of. As you read these words, somewhere in America children are being hurt. The tears of these children will not stop until our society is transformed into a place where all young people can grow up free of the fear of having pain inflicted on their bodies and minds. These children are in serious trouble. They deserve everyone's help.

BIBLIOGRAPHY

Franklin, Alfred, W., ed. *The Challenge of Child Abuse.* New York: Grune and Stratton, 1978.

Hanson, Ranae. *Institutional Abuse of Children and Youth.* New York: Haworth Press, 1982.

Kempe, C. Henry and Helfer, Ray E. *The Battered Child.* rev. enl. ed., Chicago: University of Chicago Press, 1982.

Mrazek, Patricia, and Kempe, C.H. *Sexually Abused Children and Their Families.* Elmsford, N.Y.: Pergamon, 1981.

Newberger, Eli H. *Child Abuse.* Boston: Little, Brown, 1982.

Polansky, Norman A. *Damaged Parents: An Anatomy of Child Neglect.* Chicago: University of Chicago Press, 1981.

Rush, Florence, *The Best Kept Secret; Sexual Abuse of Children.* Englewood Cliffs, N.J.: Prentice Hall, 1980.

Sloan, Irving J. *Child Abuse: Governing Laws and Legislation.* Dobbs Ferry, N.Y.: Oceana, 1981.

Thompson, Barbara C. *Child Abuse.* Independence, MO: Herald House, 1981.

Volpe, David. *Maltreatment of The School-Aged Child.* Lexington, MA: Lexington Books, 1980.

INDEX

ABOUT THE AUTHOR

ELAINE LANDAU received her B.A. from New York University and her master's degree in Library and Information Science from Pratt Institute. She worked on the editorial staff of a children's book publishing company and as a children's librarian before becoming Director of Tuckahoe Public Library in Tuckahoe, New York. She is now the Group Work Specialist for Adult Services of the New York Public Library.